"Know Thyself"

Dreams are fragile things, abiding in the realms of our subconscious mind, potent with authority and insight, resonant with a wiser, deeper perspective than our waking ego conscious can wield. To ignore them, or to diminish their importance in our lives, is to literally cut ourselves off from one of the most fertile resources we possess.

Above the entrance to the great oracle of Delphi hung the words "Know Thyself." This sage advice should strike a chord of recognition within the heart of every Witch. For if we do not embark on the journey of excavating our authentic selves, how can our magick and creativity be informed with true consciousness?

Take this journey with me—learn how your own dream symbols may correspond to the systems of tarot, collective archetypes, and shamanism. Align yourself with the waxing and waning cycles of the moon in order to enhance your dreaming experience. Awaken your intuition and imagination through ancient archetypal truths hidden in the language of your dreams. Unlock the secrets that lie within. Inform your magick. Know thyself.

KARRI ALLRICH

D1462337

About the Author

Karri Allrich is an author and artist who has studied dreams and archetypal symbology from a Jungian and magickal perspective for over twenty-five years. Karri leads an ongoing Dream Circle where she teaches the intuitive art of dream interpretation and incorporating dream symbols into ritual and magickal workings.

To Write to the Author

If you wish to contact the author or would like more information about this book, please write to the author in care of Llewellyn Worldwide and we will forward your request. Both the author and publisher appreciate hearing from you and learning of your enjoyment of this book and how it has helped you. Llewellyn Worldwide cannot guarantee that every letter written to the author can be answered, but all will be forwarded. Please write to:

Karri Allrich
℅ Llewellyn Worldwide
P.O. Box 64383, Dept. 1-56718-014-0
St. Paul, MN 55164-0383, U.S.A.

Please enclose a self-addressed stamped envelope for reply,
or $1.00 to cover costs. If outside U.S.A., enclose
international postal reply coupon.

Many of Llewellyn's authors have websites with additional information
and resources. For more information, please visit our website at
http://www.llewellyn.com

Understanding the Power of Dreams & Symbols

A WITCH'S BOOK OF DREAMS

KARRI ALLRICH

2001
Llewellyn Publications
St. Paul, Minnesota 55164-0383, U.S.A.

FIRST EDITION
First Printing, 2001

Book design and editing by Karin Simoneau
Cover art © 2001 by Karri Allrich
Cover design by Anne Marie Garrison

Library of Congress Cataloging-in-Publication Data
Allrich, Karri.
   A witch's book of dreams: understanding the power of dreams & symbols / Karri Allrich.
      p.cm.
   Includes bibliographical references and index.
   ISBN 1-56718-014-1
   1. Witchcraft. 2. Dreams—Miscellanea. 3. Archetype (Psychology)—Miscellanea. I. Title.

BF1572. D73 2001
154.6'3—dc21   00-52099

Llewellyn Worldwide does not participate in, endorse, or have any authority or responsibility concerning private business transactions between our authors and the public.

All mail addressed to the author is forwarded but the publisher cannot, unless specifically instructed by the author, give out an address or phone number.

Any Internet references contained in this work are current at publication time, but the publisher cannot guarantee that a specific location will continue to be maintained. Please refer to the publisher's website for links to authors' websites and other sources.

Llewellyn Publications
A Division of Llewellyn Worldwide, Ltd.
P.O. Box 64383, Dept. 1-56718-014-0
St. Paul, MN 55164-0383, U.S.A.
www.llewellyn.com

 Printed in the United States of America

Acknowledgments

I would like to express my deep gratitude to my editor, Karin Simoneau, for her clarity and devotion to this project. Thanks also to Nancy Mostad, Lisa Braun, and all those at Llewellyn who believe in dreams coming true. To my Dream Circle women, thank you all for your willingness to share, to laugh, and to join in the mystery of dreamtime.

Other Books by Karri Allrich

Recipes from a Vegetarian Goddess
Llewellyn Publications, 2000

For all those who dare to dream and seek to remember . . .
to reclaim the dusty fragments, polishing them with fervent ache
until they shine softly in Persephone's smile . . .
This Witch's Book of Dreams is dedicated to you.

CONTENTS

INTRODUCTION

Dreaming is a nightly occurrence, even though we may try to believe otherwise, claiming not to remember a thing, shaking off the soft nocturnal world with barely a hint of an image or lingering sensation, insisting on letting go of the night, whisking off sleep and dreams to push ourselves into consciousness and back into the busy world of daylight—of doing, making, working, talking. All external in focus, invested in performance.

As healers, intuitives, and seekers, we understand the concept of symbols, the use of sympathetic associations in the natural laws of the universe. Witches respect the unspoken truths that run beneath the apparent surface of things; the hidden realities of energy and power; the potency contained in a conscious intention; the beauty and capability of creative visualization. Well then, shouldn't we tend to our dreams as well?

Dreams are fragile gifts, abiding in the realms of our subconscious mind, rich with insight and authority, resonant with a wiser, deeper perspective than our waking ego consciousness can muster. To ignore dreams or diminish their importance in our lives is to literally cut ourselves off from one of the most fertile resources we all possess.

Indeed, within our dreams exists a deep reservoir of ancient wisdom, a pool of metaphor and symbolic energies that the celebrated Swiss psychoanalyst Carl Jung named the *Collective Unconscious*.

This resource of collective wisdom thrives within us today, collaborating with us in understanding our authentic selves. We need only activate and call forth these ancient archetypal energies to aid us in shamanic journeying, communion, and healing magick.

Above the entrance to the great oracle of Delphi hung the words "Know Thyself." This sage advice should strike a chord of recognition within the heart of every Witch. For if we do not embark on excavating our authentic selves, how can our magick and creativity be informed with true consciousness? How can our power and insight be balanced? How can we embark on healing the world when we have not yet healed ourselves?

Making a commitment to working with dreams on a regular basis opens our understanding of how we *truly* view ourselves and our world. In *A Witch's Book of Dreams,* we will examine different methods of keeping a dream journal, the core of our practice, and create a uniquely personal dream dictionary.

As we explore sample dreams, we will deepen our understanding of the power of symbols; we will learn to call upon archetypal energies to inform workings of magick and self-healing. Jung's groundbreaking concept of our inner soul twin, *Anima and Animus,* and its profound importance to growth, will be clearly explored and identified.

In chapter 4, The Importance of Shadow Work, we will delve into patterns of belief and behavior that may hinder our magick in subtle ways and blind us to the whole truth. By learning to embrace our shadow, as Witches, we learn our most valuable lesson: That by taking ownership of our unknown aspects, we truly free our energy and tap into our genuine power.

By understanding the gifts that nightmares bring to us, we learn to let go of our fears and ready ourselves to face the obstacles that shamanic journeys often toss in our path. By recognizing the symbols of our own self-limitations, we learn to face our fears and put them in their proper place, with a Witch's perspective!

In learning about mythological blueprints, we deepen our respect for dreams and begin to see the wisdom and foresight that our subconscious contains, often predicting outcomes before our waking "rational" mind can conceive them.

Introduction

We will explore how dream images may correspond to the symbols within tarot, myth, and shamanism, and how to align ourselves with the waxing and waning cycles of the moon, using intention to enhance the dreaming experience. We will awaken our intuition and imagination through ancient archetypal truths hidden in the language of dreams. We will also discover the Witch's tools of Active Imagination, Association, and Automatic Writing to expand the art of dream interpretation.

I invite you to take this journey with me through *A Witch's Book of Dreams* and tap into the power of your personal dream symbology. Unlock the secrets that lie within. Inform your magick. Know thyself.

1

UNDERSTANDING ARCHETYPES

Where do dreams come from? To answer that question, we must first understand the concept of archetypes. And to understand archetypes, we must first think about energy.

We are, each of us, essentially comprised of bundles of energy . . . energy that interacts with and connects us to what we perceive as the world around us. Everything in our universe vibrates with energy. Within and without us is an ever-pulsing exchange of this unseen force. Our body, our very being, is a collection of various energies, and Witches understand that this assemblage includes the energy of our conscious thoughts, our emotions, our intuitions, and our intentions.

Deeper within our psyche, we each contain the energy of our personal subconscious. This hidden inner awareness is a powerful source of energy, a highly charged accumulation of our past experiences, observations, emotional responses, and associations that we have personally encountered in life from birth onward.

Feeding into this personal subconscious energy within our own psyche is a deeper *collective* energy system . . . an enormous hidden ocean of shared beliefs, ancient knowledge, and powerful archetypal dynamics. Passed down from hundreds of thousands of years ago, through each successive generation, is this shared amalgam of beliefs and truths about human nature: our collective experience of what it means to be a human being, inhabiting this earth and participating in her vast matrix of interacting energy. Carl Jung (called by local townsfolk the "Warlock of Geneva"!), has identified this inherited sea of knowledge as the Collective Unconscious.

Out of this vast psychic ocean springs the human urge to create, to express, to signify. From storytelling myths, fables, cave paintings, masks, and rituals, to poetry, dance, tarot, art, festivals, and even movies, humans have invariably felt the desire to give expression to the energies living in our shared Collective Unconscious. These primal energies are known as *archetypes*, and they live within all of us.

Religion and Myth

Each one of us is part of the collective energy system that created the concept of God and Goddess; the mythic stories and images that help define life's meaning, purpose, conflicts, and truths. These timeworn myths, filled with Gods and Goddesses, all emanate from *within us*. The symbols, personalities, and metaphors are manifestations of our own energies, our very bodies, our human souls. Myth is our mirror.

Religion, for instance, is one extensive example of how humans have tried to make sense of their world and their place in it. By creating spiritual myths and systems of belief that sprang from their collective soul need to understand the great mysteries, ancient kinsmen contained their hopes and fears within a framework that reflected the spectrum of human experience and the impulse toward encountering the divine.

By creating religious mythology, humans give meaning to life's myriad questions. Throughout time, religious beliefs have comforted and nurtured humankind's need to find purpose and hope within the short expanse of their time on earth. Religion is full of archetypal energies, shared by people all over this green and blue planet. By comparing and studying the multiple religions around the world throughout the past and present, we see many connecting threads of meaning and repeated themes that are shared by all and are deeply archetypal. Yet another reason to support the growing cry for tolerance and acceptance of diversity.

Archetypes in Fairy Tales

Archetypes are the myriad faces of human impulse, behavior patterns, and psychological truths. We respond in recognition, resonating within our very bones, because these myths contain our own reflections. Ever since early childhood we were able to identify with the archetypal truths revealed to us in fairy tales, nursery rhymes, myths of Gods and Goddesses, religious stories of creation and rebirth. Stories that attempted to teach us about love, fear, courage, creation, power, death, and renewal.

In our youth, for instance, we all inherently recognized and laughed at the Clown archetype, seeing our own foolish (naive) selves reflected in his antics. We grew quiet with anticipation listening to stories of the terrifying fire-breathing Dragon who lived in the dank dripping cave, or the scary ugly beast that lived in the dark woods . . . or even worse, under the bed!

We felt heartened by the brave Knight in armor who set out on his quest for justice, and felt awe for the mysterious Priestess, the Lady of the Lake, who kept the sacred sword Excalibur hidden beneath the misted Avalon waters. As children we all grew up with such legends and fairy-tale images, fables and mythical stories. Even at an innocent young age we somehow sensed the truths revealed within the characters and tales of our cultural mythologies.

Finding Your Roots

I was born of Scottish-Irish blood, never knowing my birth father, living with my working mother and rather harrowing grandparents. Eventually my mother remarried and I was whisked off into a very Americanized middle-class neighborhood, hiding my Witchy tendencies as best I could, no longer an only child with the freedom to roam the fields and nearby woods. I was trapped in suburbia.

My craving for mythology and lost roots led me to books, exploring with utter awe the stories of King Arthur, Merlin and Nimue, the quest for the Holy Grail, Morgaine and the Mists of Avalon, Herne, the Green Man, Robin Hood, the Selkie, sirens, the magical

Beauty and the Beast, and Rhiannon the Shapeshifter. These tales filled my heart with longing and touched upon a deepening sense of inner knowing. I recognized that I had somehow, in these stories, found my true home. That's the way archetypes work; they resonate within the very core of our being. Tales of Merlin and magick echoed within my ancestral taproots. The stories and myths that reverberate within you will reflect your own cultural bent.

It is also enlightening to study other cultures, time periods, and belief systems; often we are attracted to the beauty of another's culture. The Lakota, North American Plains People, have a poetic spirituality that attracted me for several years when I lived out West. As I came to realize the similarities it shared with the Celtic and Druid paths, I felt that I needed to return to my own beginnings with a fresh eye and honor my own ancestors.

Find your personal roots within your heritage and you will discover a treasure chest of stories, legends, and symbols that speak uniquely to you.

Universal Archetypes

As we study myth and learn about the universality of many symbols, we begin to notice that certain archetypes are so powerful that they emerge within many differing belief systems. The universal appeal of tarot reminds us of this fact. Every culture shares a Fool archetype: an innocent living on the fringe, an outsider people laugh at but learn from; for the Fool has his own logic and wisdom. In the North American Plains Lakota tribe, for instance, the *Heyoka* fulfills this role; doing things backward, he makes the people laugh as he plays the clown. But he is teaching them spiritual lessons while they are busy laughing.

Another widespread example is the archetype of the Wise One and the Hermit. Most cultures have solitary Healers: Medicine Men and Women trained in the Old Folk Ways, rich in folk wisdom, that the tribe or people turn to for healing and guidance. Every human understands the universal archetype of the patriarch: king, chief, and leader. We all know the familiar patterns of the heroic youth, the brave warrior, the virginal maiden, the protective mother, the passionate lover, and the divinely radiant newborn baby. These types are collectively shared in our human experience.

All cultures have their own versions of a creation myth and stories about the earth, her seasons and creatures. All share tales of jealousy, sacrifice, power, honor, and enlightenment. There certainly may be differences in priorities and what individual cultures hold in high esteem. Our western consumer culture values upward mobility, youth, and material gain, while older European cultures may value extended family and have a deeper respect for old age. But amidst the differences in every tribe and culture, each belief system, there are communal truths about human nature, character struggles, and soul yearnings that are universal.

We express these similarities through dreams, art, and music, in symbols and archetypes.

In our personal dreamscape we may dream of our familiar childhood home, for instance, and of finding an unknown set of stairs that takes us into a marvelous new room. We might absorb every detail of the color, the windows, the furnishings, and feel the deep sense of individual revelation in discovering this beautiful new space. It feels very unique to us, and we may be tempted to literalize the dream and make it merely a personal wish, a fantasy for new living quarters.

But this dream is also archetypal. The archetype is the experience. For the experience of discovering a new "room" is symbolic of realizing a new consciousness, new psychic space within our original self (childhood home), and this experience is *universal*. It symbolizes growth, moving up, expanding into a new level of awareness. It is this *experience* of growth into new awareness that is archetypal.

Whether the house you dream of is a brick mansion or a pup tent, the home is the container of the self, and a "new room" is growth, new awareness within. I have a good friend who recently dreamt of flying in her new teepee. She felt exhilarated and adventurous. In the past, she had often dreamt of her childhood brick home on a manicured street. I told her that I was very excited about her soaring teepee! She was obviously leaving behind her past self and taking off on a new flight of freedom. Her home/self was now portable, even airborne, allowing her to navigate into her future with ease.

Another classic archetypal example might be a falling dream. You may dream an intensely vivid dream about climbing up the side of a mountain and feel every detail of the rock and stone face; it may even be a path you are personally familiar with, a trail you know well. Suddenly you lose your footing and begin to slip. You start falling backward and tumbling; your heart is beating faster and the surge of adrenaline wakes you up in a cold sweat. You might be tempted to think of the dream in very personalized way, hinting at your fear of heights or this particularly tough trail, or recalling a past experience you once had. But the sensation of climbing, slipping, and falling is an archetypal experience. The perception of feeling unfounded, faltering in one's progress, is universal. And that is what the dream is about. The shared collective experience of falling short. Slipping up. It is important that we step back from our dreams and examine the overall experience . . . it may reflect the essential theme of our life at that moment.

Media Archetypes:
Recognizing Myth in Contemporary Life

As Witches, we may easily recognize archetypal wisdom when we gaze at tarot cards. But do we also realize, while sitting in a darkened public theater watching a film such as *Braveheart*, that we are participating in a *collective experience* of archetypal energies? Sitting together in the audience, we are all stirred deeply by recognizing the power of William Wallace's archetypal hero. Sharing in his story of courage and bravery in the face of oppression infuses us with the fire of this archetypal heroic energy. We all participate in it.

Film and television portray many archetypes to our collective culture, perhaps on a scale unparalleled in our history, reaching millions of viewers. When we respond to an image on the screen, we are reacting to the power of that particular archetype, activating its energy within our own consciousness. If we feel a deep response to the film's character or the pattern of the story, it clues our subconscious to identify with and project that same character or pattern onto the actor, recognizing an aspect of ourselves in the story and film.

This explains the phenomenon of several people all identifying with the same past life figure! I know more than one person who believes they were actually Cleopatra in a previous life. (And I have heard of several who believe they were Braveheart, including a housewife and mother of three living in Iowa.) I personally suspect that these past life "feelings" are more indicative of an archetypal identification than an actual past life incarnation.

One clue here is the *fame* of the historic figure. History creates myths from a mixture of fact, exaggeration, archetype, and psychological patterns. The myths live on, evolve, and expand over time, colored by the storytellers. We look back and cannot help but identify with certain heroes and figures portrayed in the past. Our identification is with the archetypal energy.

I suspect a few readers are now a bit displeased. No, I do not reject the concept of reincarnation, I am intrigued by it, as was my hero, Carl Jung. But there are way too many people in modern America who believe they were once the same famous figure! As unromantic as it may seem, chances are, if we have lived before, we weren't anyone famous.

Think twice before you decide that your powerful sense of identification or familiarity with a famous figure in history indicates a past life. It is far more likely, in my humble opinion, that you are responding to the archetype itself, identifying with its *energy*, similar to when we feel a kinship to certain Goddesses and Gods. We understand that we are invoking the energy inherent in their archetype, tapping into the power of it, bringing the dynamics of the Goddess or God into being. Many practitioners may believe that the Gods and Goddesses literally do exist, and I am not here to argue with that viewpoint, only to offer my opinion that it is the very *energy* itself we are encountering. And that energy is eternal. For me, that does not diminish the mystery of it all, but helps to clarify my understanding of divine energy, archetypal power, and magick.

Contemporary Types

Because of our identifications and psychological projections, familiar public figures, actors, and artists from film and television may show up in our dreams as representations of the archetypal. This certainly makes sense: in these postmodern days we seldom sit around the hearth fire sharing spoken tales of the days of old, and Greek and Roman myth may only be taught briefly in school, so it is unlikely that we will dream of Zeus or Artemis. But the ever-pervasive media provides us with powerful contemporary motifs of modern day myths, reflecting ancient archetypal energies in a contemporary fashion.

Masculine Archetypal Energies

Our two-thousand-year-old patriarchal (Judeo-Christian) culture elevates and exalts the masculine father archetypes of the powerful King, the fearless Warrior, and the almighty vengeful Sky God, all forces of action, power, heroism and sacrifice, judgment and law; embodying the attributes of intellect and rationality, valuing mind over matter and instinct. This elevation and glorification is evident all around us, from our grand steepled churches to our complex government, from the structure of social inequalities to the elaborate sports arenas, from the CEO of worldwide corporations down to the competitive lessons taught in our school classrooms.

In contemporary myth, the Western film genre is a timeless example of man's struggle with these patriarchal issues of power, greed, and heroism, with its *Good Guy versus the Bad Guy* themes. Classic shadow projection!

George Lucas took these classic masculine themes of the American West into the space age with his futuristic series *Star Wars;* archetypal good versus evil. Patriarchal power is represented by the empire ruled by an aging emperor. Darth Vadar, representing a man in power who is seduced by his dark shadow side, becomes increasingly more machine and less human, less soulful—Lucas' warning about elevating technology above the values of empathy, compassion, and human life.

Luke Skywalker is the quintessential young hero: idealistic and called to adventure. Han Solo is the perfect reluctant hero, a bit jaded and world-weary. He has resisted patriarchal values in his own wisecracking way, rejecting the system in his lone cowboy pursuits. Princess Leah might have been the typical helpless heroine needing a fairy-tale rescue, but thankfully Lucas imbued her with intelligence and leadership. She then becomes a more fleshed out twin (literally the Anima) for both Luke and Han.

Comics and computer games are also full of superheroes who battle similar "evils" and struggle with the inhumanity inherent in a corporate culture, providing archetypal myths for an entire subculture of avid fans and collectors.

The Father Archetypes

As Witches, we may turn to the system of tarot to recognize these masculine archetypes. Such patriarchal energies are portrayed in the Emperor card, a card of power and protection, reason and conviction. The four King cards are also variations of the fatherly archetype. The King of Wands is an excellent example; he is a leader and a strategist, an adventurer, fiery and conflictual.

In our dreams, we may encounter such energies as a gray-bearded man, a tyrant, a father figure, a wise professor, or a fearless warrior-soldier. Often the masculine figure will be mythic or famous, a clue to his archetypal symbolism.

As a young woman, I once had a dream about Superman himself . . . revealing an obvious unconscious desire to be rescued and swept off my feet! I had not yet developed my own heroic side. This dream showed me that I was remaining passive in my life, wishing for a superhero to arrive. Upon contemplation, I decided instead to rescue myself!

When we encounter such archetypal energy in a dream, we must seek to understand the message.

As you encounter the masculine in a dream, ask yourself how this masculine figure affects you. Examine how his energy works within

9

the dream. What emotion does he trigger? It may be a clue to understanding your own participation in such an attitude, a warning of such a tendency within yourself. Or it may be revealing collective influence upon your spirit.

If the persona of the archetype is indeed "bigger than life," look into the mythic story he is a part of. His actions in the story may predict just where his influence is headed and what archetypal patterns may be emerging in your life. Our subconscious recognizes the overall patterns of specific behaviors and can foretell where we might be headed, even if we do not consciously see it. If you dream of Darth Vadar, for example, you may be approaching a confrontation with your own inherited father/shadow, losing touch with your vulnerability in favor of power and protection within the prevailing system.

The Son Archetypes

The son archetypes are represented in tarot within the major arcana's Lover (symbolizing Eros, mercurial and magnetic), and in the Knight cards, representing the heroic, romantic, idealistic, or volatile nature of youth. These are very different energies from the power-based father/patriarchal archetypes. One of my personal favorites is the archetypal Trickster, or Messenger. Embodied by the Magician card in tarot, this form of masculine energy is personified in myth as the figure of Hermes, or Mercury, the traveler. He is "the one who travels between two worlds," like quicksilver, able to understand both the language of mortals and the language of the Gods.

Sting, the English musician/songwriter/actor, comes to mind as personifying this Hermes archetype. Mining the depths of Shakespeare and philosophy, Jungian psychology and myth, Sting takes his inspiration from the classics and infuses his lyrics and music with the stuff of the Gods, layering messages and meaning, rich in complexity, yet accessible.

For years, Sting has appeared in my own dreams as this archetype, offering me books, messages, and elucidation, often in ancient writing. The next day in waking life, I might be suddenly drawn to a certain book or begin thinking about a new concept in my work, feeling as if Sting/Hermes himself was standing behind my shoulder, guiding me toward certain titles, urging me toward exploring new ideas. This is archetypal energy at work!

Another son archetype is the Lover . . . the man who values women, wine, and pleasure, also known as Dionysos. In the myth of Dionysos, we see a father's son rebel against the law and values of the Sky God's system. This boy becomes a poet and musician, wanderer, lover of many women, seeking ecstasy and transcendence through music, wine, and dance.

American rock star and poet Jim Morrison, member of the 1960s band The Doors, and Michael Hutchence, of the Australian band INXS, both personified and identified with this powerful and seductive archetype. Jim Morrison even had a militaristic, Zeuslike father who was involved in the Vietnam war. In the myth of Dionysos, the lover himself is destroyed in the end, torn to shreds, devoured by raging hunger and passion. Both Morrison and Hutchence paid a personal price for courting this archetype in the public arena. The powerful energy of this archetype, intensified by the collective's participation in their own mass projection of it, ended up literally destroying them both. Each died at a young age; Jim at twenty-seven and Michael at thirty-seven, their deaths surrounded in mystery and speculation, the press hungry for details and dirt. Our Sky God culture is poorer from the loss of these two gifted Dionysian men, lovers of women and the Goddess. If ever a man embodied Herne, the Horned One's energy, and Dionysos, these two did. I miss them both.

In the section on the Animus, the masculine soul twin revealed in women's dreams, I further discuss the archetype of the Lover, the Daimon who fuels a woman's passion. This secret Daimon Lover (the counterpart to a man's muse, the one who fills women with passion and creative fire) within a women's psyche is the source of creativity, much like a man's muse, inspiring a woman toward feelings of drive and enthusiasm.

As mentioned previously, in tarot we are able to see the son archetypes portrayed in the Knight cards of the four suits. The

Knight of Wands, for instance, is impulsive and poised, following the inspirational fire of his many ideas. He is changeable and mobile. Spanish actor Antonio Banderas smolders with the fire of this archetype, most notably in the film *Desperado*.

In the Knight of Cups we see the romantic aspect of the male psyche, sensitive and motivated by love. This archetype is idealistic and mirrors back to us all the naive hopes and dreams that youth pursues with genuine passion and heart, personified by Luke Skywalker in *Star Wars*. In *A Walk in the Clouds, Say Anything,* and *Little Voice*, Keanu Reeves, John Cusack, and Ewan MacGregor, respectively, bring the love and gentleness of the Knight of Cups to their quiet heroism.

Often archetypes are combined, especially in the son archetype of the outlaw, the bad boy, the rebel. He may be fiery and confrontational and have the impulsiveness of Mars, the Warrior archetype, yet he may also contain a vulnerability, a sweetness betraying the Lover or even the Idealist. Our culture loves this new reluctant hero archetype—the boy-man who remains a bit irresponsible, who bucks the system, rebelling against the patriarchal expectations. Actors Brad Pitt, Mark Wahlberg, Johnny Depp, and George Clooney are all examples of the more complex antiheroes who contain both dark and light, and wrestle with collective demons for us.

Feminine Archetypal Energies

As women, and Witches, we long for portrayals of powerful women heroines in film, but alas, they are few and far between. Archetypal images of women in film are too often portrayed within the standard prototypes of wife and mother, classic bitch, or damsel in distress. Rare is the female who contains both beauty and strength, fire and imagination.

One exception is the character of Annie Savoy in *Bull Durham*, played beautifully by Susan Sarandon; Annie is a feisty mystical Aphrodite archetype, secure in her sensuality and female power. As the Goddess of love, poetry, and art, this archetype urges us to find power in our sexuality, to nurture beauty in our lives, to express our spirit through the arts—whether it be painting, poetry, or love. (Or in Annie's case, even baseball!) Another example is the role of Erin Brockovich, played by Julia Roberts; Erin is a woman who is unafraid of expressing her sexuality and her determination. A potent combination.

Another exception is in the film *Practical Magic*. In this movie, the two Witchy aunts are affectionately portrayed by Dianne Wiest and Stockard Channing. A pair of wise crones, full of life, humor, and eccentricity, living outside the collective value system, whipping up midnight margaritas.

In the Cinderella remake *Ever After*, Drew Barrymore plays a maiden with guts and problem-solving skills, bringing a strong feminist slant to the familiar fairy tale. And Christina Ricci is radiant as the young Katrina Von Tassel in Tim Burton's stunning ode to gothic horror *Sleepy Hollow*, protecting her love with the power of her Craft. So there is hope!

In tarot we find that the court cards depicting Queens are perfect examples of strong feminine archetypes. The Queen of Swords is a noble and just illustration. Cool and independent, she correlates with the Athena archetype in Greek myth, able to cut through deception with her sword of truth and clarity. The character of Dana Scully in the wildly successful television series *The X-Files* is the epitome of the Athena archetype, played with cool panache by actress Gillian Anderson. A breath of fresh air in a broadcast sea of one-dimensional female characters.

Contrasting the levelheaded coolness of the Queen of Swords is the Queen of Cups, whose still waters run deep. She is magnetic and intuitive, a deep well of feminine mystery. The Priestess archetype. Not often portrayed for us in film or television. She is the elusive Lady of the Lake, or perhaps the magnetic Gnostic, Mary Magdalene.

Another archetypal example of the feminine is the Crone, Wise Woman, Witch, and Healer. The "One Who Knows." She personifies the ancient connection with earth energy and true power—power not from brute force, but from working in harmony with the earth's natural energy cycles. The power of healing.

This archetype is very threatening to a patriarchal-based culture such as ours, which emphasizes domination and technology. Earth knowledge and intuition are devalued, even ridiculed. The once proud archetype of the Witch and Healer, or Medicine Woman, has been watered down in disrespect to cartoony Witches flying on brooms and green-faced hags with warts. At best, she is the one-dimensional Glenda the Good Witch or Samantha twitching her pert nose.

Waking the Witch

In working with people's dreams and observing popular culture, I have come to feel that the powerful Witch or Goddess is returning to the Collective Unconscious in her positive form. Many women are dreaming of dark emerging Earth Goddesses or swimming in the aqua sea with beautiful warm-blooded whales, or even making love to female figures. These dreams reflect a return of the Goddess values, an awakening of the ancient feminine. Even the global increase of Virgin Mary sightings are a positive sign that the Divine Feminine is returning. The widespread renewed interest in the Goddess at this turn of the millennium mirrors the archetypal energy of our Mother Earth herself, trying to nudge us all awake . . . before it's too late.

Universal Archetypes

No matter which culture we are born into, we will have stories and myths that reflect universal human truths and archetypal energies. All cultures have their depictions, from masks and ritualistic enactments and dances, to cave paintings, drawings, and sculpture, to sacred writings and fables about human issues (myths about greed, mercy, change, jealousy, compassion, loss, sex, power, innocence, death, and rebirth). Tarot decks and animal totems, fetishes and costumes are all powerful embodiments of these archetypal energies. Films and television shows (*Star Wars* and *The X-Files*, for example) are modern-day versions of mythmaking that affect people on an enormous collective scale.

In beginning the process of dream work, we are tapping into our personal subconscious in order to understand the underpinnings of our own journeys. We are reflecting upon our choices of behavior and values and examining the urge and power of our energies.

As we work with our dreams, we sense the presence of the Collective Unconscious poking at our awareness, giving us a deeper set of choices to ponder.

What parts of myself are truly authentic to me?
What parts have I adopted from the pressure
of the societal collective to conform?
Am I true to myself in the face of family
and cultural pressures?

The path we are on through dream work is a path to awareness, to wholeness, to integration—to authentic personal power.

Archetypes in Film

Once you become familiar with archetypal energies and how they emerge in contemporary culture, it might be interesting to view a few movies with strong archetypal characters and mythic structure. Notice which archetypes you respond to, both positively and negatively. The positive attraction you feel toward an archetype may reveal a desire to integrate that energy into your own life and an identification with the mythic journey of the character. A strong repulsion to a particular figure often indicates a recognition of your shadow self, a hidden aspect you are reluctant to express.

I've listed a few contemporary films below that feature definitive archetypes or mythic journeys.

Braveheart, Bull Durham, Casablanca, The Crying Game, Dances with Wolves, Don Juan DeMarco, Edward Scissorhands, Ever After, Excalibur, Fargo, Fatal Attraction, Fight Club, First Knight, Gladiator, Holy Smoke, L.A. Confidential, The Last of the Mohicans, Legends of the Fall, Local Hero, Magnolia, The Matrix, Merlin, The Piano,

Powwow Highway, Practical Magic, The Princess Bride, The Quick and the Dead, Raiders of the Lost Ark, The Silence of the Lambs, The Sixth Sense, Sleepy Hollow, Sling Blade, Star Wars trilogy, Thelma and Louise, The Thin Red Line, Thunderheart, Twelve Monkeys, Unforgiven, The Usual Suspects, The X-Files

2

The Language of Symbols

Witches understand symbolic language. They know that the hidden meanings of symbols and objects, rituals and visions is what gives power to their magick. The underlying truths in the natural world feed their imagination and inspire them to think symbolically. To enter into the realm of the Witch is to enter into a preverbal world of intuition, image, metaphor, and instinct.

As we enter into a dream to interpret it, we must think symbolically. We must learn to see the aspects in our dream as elements of ourselves and the subconscious mind.

Characters as Aspects of Yourself

People who appear in your dream, be they family members, children, strangers, celebrities, or friends, are all an aspect of you. Think of every character in your dream as if holding a mirror, reflecting back to you an aspect or part of your true self.

The Inner Child

A child in a dream might reflect your younger self, your childhood innocence, your own Inner Child archetype. The child may have a message for you, prompting you to look back into your past and remember a younger aspect of yourself that you have forgotten or left behind. Perhaps you need to get reacquainted with your child self. Often, your younger self will appear in a dream in order to heal an aspect of your psyche that was wounded in childhood.

My husband, an accomplished visual artist, long ago endeavored to be a writer. As a boy he had spent countless hours at his manual typewriter banging out stories for his friends. As an adult, he had not considered the possibility of writing for more than twenty years. In his early forties, he had the following dream that perfectly illustrates this concept of reclaiming discarded aspects of yourself.

> *I am standing in a hallway that is lined with windows. A young boy wearing a striped tee shirt suddenly rides up on a bicycle. He is towing a wagon behind him. He gets off the bike and walks back to the wagon, reaches in, and picks up a shiny silver key. Handing it to me, he says, "This is for you." I take the key and suddenly find myself in a room that feels familiar. I look around and notice a small wooden box sitting on the floor in the center of the room. I approach the box and open it with the key. Inside is a piece of paper, folded in quarters. Opening it up, I see that there is writing on it and I take it over to the light of the window in order to see it more clearly. The writing is blurry at first, but after a while I am able to read it. I feel as if I am on the verge of understanding the written message when I wake up. (I was unable to remember any of the words I'd read.)*

The dreamer is standing in a hallway, symbolizing a passage, a transition. There are windows lighting the hallway, indicating he is aware, conscious that he is in this transitional position. The child approaching him on the bike is his younger self. (The clue is the striped tee shirt the dreamer recognized as one he once wore.) The boy is pulling a wagon, which holds a silver key. The wagon is the symbol of how we carry things along with us on our life's journey. His younger self had carried along this key for him all these years! The key is silver, the metal of intuition, moonlight, and dreams. Then the dreamer finds himself in a familiar room. This is a part of himself he once inhabited. He spies the box, a forgotten treasure chest, something he locked away in himself and left behind a long time ago. There is a message inside, on paper, folded in quarters. This is significant; the paper, of course, relates to his desire to write. The folds reveal the sacred number four—the equal cross: balance, pairs, opposites, the four directions. This message is about these attributes of four. He cannot read the writing at first. The dream message isn't clear to him yet. But he brings it over to the light of the window, to see better. He is bringing the message to conscious-ness and throwing "light on the subject." He begins to understand the message. Illumination!

The dreamer had this dream at midlife. His younger self came to remind him that his youthful desires *held the key* for him at this time of transition. His intuition (the silver key) was the means to unlocking this information that he had hidden away for a long time. The dreamer began to think about his childhood dream of writing again. After decades of putting that aspiration aside, he opened the locked box, his contained desire to be a writer, and brought it to light.

Today, as well as painting, he has been writing nonfiction and fic-tion ever since that dream. He has a found a greater sense of bal-ance in his life, giving equal time to his opposite desires of expres-sion: writing and painting; verbal and visual. The dreamer had been at a crossroads and had allowed his younger self to guide him to a greater sense of balance in his creativity.

Another example of how the Inner Child archetype may appear to us in order to bring about healing and change is illustrated in the following dream that I had.

I am standing in a room that feels unfamiliar to me, yet I "know" that it is a room in my own house. A young girl appears in front of me; she is about six years old. I focus in on her, and slowly realize that I am looking at my younger girlish self. Her hair is permed and curly, unnatural, and she wears a pink barrette in it. Her dress is overly feminine, like a stiff party dress. She looks a little uncomfortable, quite fid-gety. Her patent leather shoes are pinching. Suddenly I understand what she needs from me. I grab a comb and begin combing out her hair, gently. As I comb it, the awful perm begins to relax, and her hair returns to its natural fine straightness. It is shiny and silky. I help her get out of the party dress and shiny shoes, and into a simple tee shirt and jeans. She is barefoot. I pull her hair loosely back into a pony-tail. She turns and smiles at me. "Go play," I tell her, and pat her on the behind as she turns and runs off.

This was a lucid dream experience I had during bodywork. I was quite surprised at the emotions triggered by the appearance of my young girl self. In the dream she appears in a room that is unfamiliar and yet somehow I understand that this room is a part of my house, myself. This new space symbolizes a new aspect, new awareness. The young girl/self had come to me so I might return to my childhood and reclaim her true spirit.

Complex issues of self-esteem, ideal beauty, and the strive for perfection haunt a lot of women in this culture. In this dream I was able to go back and acknowledge her discomfort with the constricting dress and shoes, the pressure to conform to a narrow expression of femininity. In symbolically combing out the unnatural home perm, I was reclaiming my younger self, "combing out" the inherent message that she was not good enough, not pretty enough, without altering her natural appearance. Our culture's collective expectation of femininity, symbolized by the frilly party dress and rigid shoes, was removed and replaced with simple clothing that allowed the little girl to run free, uninhibited, true to her own spirit. Unencumbered now to consciously form her own ideas about true femininity; no longer under the pressure to conform to collective standards.

If a child appears in one of your dreams, welcome him or her. Pay attention to their message. They may be offering you an opportunity to heal, to reclaim, to rediscover some lost or wounded aspect of yourself. And this is a marvelous gift.

People as Symbols

The temptation with dreams is to literalize the characters within your dreamscape, believing that family members, friends, or coworkers, for example, are the same people they are in waking life. It is difficult and challenging to pull away from that persuasion and realize that *each person in the dream is an aspect of yourself.* It takes practice. If you dream of a celebrity, someone famous, a film star, for instance, it's easier to accept that this "star" is a symbolic projection of some aspect within your own self, because in waking life you do not literally encounter this person. (Unless, of course, you happen to run in celebrity circles with the rich and famous!)

A woman dreamer I know had recurring dreams about encountering a famous actress. The actress would haunt her dreams, lurking on the edges of her dreamscape:

> *I had another strange dream about (this actress). She was there in my yard, watching me, and I felt as if she was trying to tell me something. I felt very uneasy.*

This actress is talented, respected, and quite beautiful. She lives in the country, away from Hollywood, riding her horses and taking care of her family and farm. She also carries a lingering sadness about her, a wistfulness that colors her gaze and speech with a rueful bittersweet quality. I saw this same somber quality in the dreamer, though she would never admit to it. She always joked and put on a "happy face." Her dreams of the melancholy actress were attempting to expose her shadow, her own unknown and unnamed aspect; in this case, her underlying tendency toward depression, which she habitually covered up with her outgoing humor and smile, *acting* as if she had no struggle with despondency. Her dreams of the actress were dreams about her own unacknowledged sadness; a quality she did not want to admit to in herself; a revelation she wished to mask. In order to maintain the status quo, she "acted" the part of a happy woman, denying her underlying depression. When we try to avoid the truths about ourselves, our dreams will gently show us the actuality. And if we refuse to learn, the images become stronger and more graphic.

Dreaming of Family

Thinking in symbolic terms can get a little sticky when we dream of a family member, as it is all too tempting to regard the family member as exactly who they are. Strong emotions are often stirred up just thinking about our families. We all have very active impressions of our place within the family structure, and relationships can feel highly charged.

Remember that each person in your dream reflects an aspect of yourself. When dreaming of a family member, think of what this person represents to you. Often a family member will embody the *relationship* you share; for instance, if you engage in a struggle for power in your relationship with your brother, this struggle may be represented by his presence in your dream. He *is* the power struggle. If your aunt is very competitive, she will represent this aspect in yourself. If your grandfather is very authoritarian, he will represent his influence on your own tendencies toward control and leadership.

Tune in to your emotions surrounding a person's emergence in your dream. Make note of what you *feel*. This will clue you in to what the dream is really about. If you dream of your mother or father, examine what aspects of your parents you may have internalized. Do you admire what they stand for, or are you struggling against their value system?

As we grow out of our childhood, we internalize many lessons and attitudes (both positive and negative) that our parents taught us, by words and by example. Often their value system, their moral point of view, and their emotional and psychological traits will seep into our own. Each family system contains its own unique code of behavior and expectations.

As young adults we begin to sift through our own perceptions, values, and goals, choosing what belongs to us and discarding that which no longer "fits" us. Life experience begins to make an impression, and we form our own sense of autonomy, learning from our mistakes and shaping our own opinions about life. We may indeed outgrow our family system. This is especially common with independent thinkers, artists, creatives, and Witches; anyone who pursues their own individual path toward authenticity.

If you were an impressionable child, eager to please, you may find that as you grow more independent in your life, you begin having dreams about your family, parents, or one parent. Your subconscious may be urging you to be more attentive to the choices you make and how you define yourself. A parent's appearance in your dream may symbolize this struggle for differentiation.

Do you truly share the same values, the same concepts of what it means to be a woman or a man in this world? Is your parents' model befitting you today, or are you breaking away from familial patterns to explore new territory? The following dream illustrates one dreamer's struggle to overcome her sense of responsibility to her parents and find her own way in life.

> *I am driving down a street in Mexico, and there are other people in my car; they keep changing. Sometimes it is my parents, and sometimes it is two girls. I see an old friend from high school by the side of the road, waving. I pull over and stop to talk to him.*
>
> *We discuss the sad fact that a baby elephant has been born, and is lost; I am trying to find it. I go back to my car and somehow I feel as if I am "saving" or helping my parents.*
>
> *I kick the two girls out of the car in order to make room for my parents. My Dad is sitting at the wheel and has a Mexican baby on his lap, a little girl. He moves over for me to take the wheel. The baby remains and is now sitting on my lap, at the steering wheel. I drive and have to maneuver around dangerous curves and sudden crevasses. It is scary and I am not sure we're going to make it. We are bounced around, but somehow I am able to control the car.*

The dreamer is in new territory; Mexico represents the unfamiliar. She is driving, progressing in her life. Riding along with her are two girls and her parents. She is bringing her parents (and all they represent to her) along on her journey, as well as two feminine shadow aspects of herself. The girls may represent two alternative or conflictual desires she once had, or two undeveloped aspects of her girl self.

When the dreamer pushes the girls out of the car in order to make room for her parents, she is discarding dual feminine aspects of herself, or unacknowledged shadow desires, in order to accommodate her parents. Accommodation is the word that comes to mind strongly here. The dreamer is being shown that she got rid of these parts of herself and took on responsibility to her internalized parents instead.

When she pulls the car over to talk to her high-school friend, we find a clue as to when this accommodation began in her life: high school. At that time she also "lost" her baby elephant, perhaps symbolizing the loss of some newborn instinct, or the dreamer's innocence. The infant elephant, being rather sweet, quiet, needing guidance, may indicate her own tentative natural instinct, her naiveté. The dreamer now mourns its loss and desires to somehow retrieve it. Perhaps her masculine side, her Animus (the kind male friend) will be able to help her find this lost sense of instinct/innocence.

When the dreamer returns to her car (her journey), her father has been at the wheel. His influence is guiding her still. He holds a baby in his lap, a little Mexican girl. The baby symbolizes a new sense of self being born within the dreamer, a new guise of her femininity, vulnerable and unfamiliar to her.

As the dreamer slides into the driver's seat, she regains control of her direction; she is now behind the wheel of her car with the baby on her lap. She is moving ahead, making progress with the help of this brand new feminine presence at the wheel with her. The roads on her journey are challenging and feel dangerous, but she is able to handle the car.

This new direction feels unsafe and unpredictable, and the dreamer is uncertain about whether or not she'll be able to handle it all, but she does! She may feel a little jolted by life, "bounced around," but she pays attention and manages just fine.

Another dream that touches upon the dominion of parents and restraint is the following nightmare that graphically symbolized this dreamer's dilemma with her mother's (and grandmother's) influence and control.

I am in a diner, sitting in a booth, waiting to eat. My mother and my grandmother are sitting across from me. The waitress brings several plates of food over to our table and I look at all the dishes, trying to decide if any of them look appetizing to me. They don't. I tell my mother and grandmother that I am not hungry. They begin picking at the food and holding up spoonfuls to me across the table, trying to put the spoon into my mouth as if I am an infant. I feel nauseous. I push their hands away. Then my mother arises and takes out a tool bag. She opens it and pulls out surgical instruments and tools, moving over behind where I am sitting. I am worried about this.

She cuts into my scalp with a sharp scalpel and lifts off the top of my skull, pulling it aside as if it is merely a lid. She then begins to "operate" on my head, almost in electrical terms; soldering and cutting, rewiring, and using a screwdriver. It is horrifying. I am panicked. I say out loud, "I'm not sure you are qualified to do this!" I wake up in a cold sweat.

The dreamer is a woman in her mid-twenties. In her dream she is obviously struggling with her maternal familial influences. The diner represents that which feeds the collective. (She is not at her own dining table, she is at a *public* dining booth.) Her mother and grandmother fit in well with the collective, comfortable with the food that the waitress brings over to the table. There is a lot of it. Food represents that which nourishes us and feeds our spirit, our growth, whether it be ideas, "food for thought," or nurturing elements. The dreamer rejects the "food" they offer her. It does not appeal to her. She is resisting the ideas and the ideals that her family/mother feed to her, and the collective pressures to accept what the culture (symbolized by the waitress) offers to women.

When the dreamer refuses to swallow these ideas, her mother rises to the occasion. She brings out her "tool kit" and begins to surgically invade and manipulate the dreamer's mind. This is all about control, and I would intuit that the actual technique used by this mother is passive-aggressive. (The clue is that after the daughter has refused the food, the mother moves *behind* the daughter, out of sight, approaching her from the back.)

Here she violates the dreamer's mind and spirit (cutting into her head), fiddles with her energy circuit (wiring), burns her (soldering), and screws around with her mind (the screwdriver). What symbolism!

The dreamer is panicked, feeling vulnerable and exposed. She wonders if her mother is actually "qualified" to screw with her head. She understands the potential for damage. The dreamer feels powerless to stop her mother's need for control.

This definitive nightmare was a turning point in the growth of the dreamer. She began to psychically protect herself and her spirit, and gradually worked to free her soul from the invasive control of her mother.

Anima and Animus: Our Soul Twin

Perhaps the most frequently asked question in Dream Circle is, "What does this man in my dream represent?" Women who are happily married or involved in a committed relationship may feel as if they are "cheating" on their partners when they dream sexy dreams of attractive, kind, and strong men; men who are most definitely *not* their partner. They may blush or laugh nervously as they reveal the erotic charge in the dream; the electricity of his touch, the depth in his soulful eyes.

What these women are experiencing is an encounter with their Animus, which Carl Jung recognized as the inner soul twin. Within a woman exists a masculine energy, a male counterpart to her inherent femininity. As in all of nature, within each of us there exists duality: feminine and masculine energies, dark and light, contractive and expansive, below and above. In women we find the masculine soul twin and call it Animus; in men we see the twin as his feminine Anima. As we mature in life we begin to encounter our soul twin in dreams, and rarely are we disinterested. Our twin is fascinating, mysterious, alluring, sometimes even dangerous.

In accepting that we are on a journey toward wholeness, toward integration of self, toward authenticity, we acknowledge that there are unknown and unrealized aspects within us. Jung defines these unknown aspects as the shadow. Not merely the "dark" part of us, the shadow encompasses all that remains unknown to our conscious ego: our unfulfilled talents, our unexpressed traits, the denied and discarded parts of ourselves. Our Anima or Animus is an aspect of this shadow territory. As women we must begin to explore our inner masculine energy if we are to truly become whole. As men, the need is to realize the inner feminine and integrate her into full awareness.

The function of the Animus figure in women's dreams is to help her develop her creativity and assist her in bringing her thoughts and ideas out into the light of the world. Women's inherent feminine way is to be receptive, intuitive, adept at the art of "being," at one with the natural flow of nature. Think of the moon and the subtle energies she represents.

These traits are all positive (even though they may not be celebrated in this culture), yet in order to move into wholeness and integration, a woman's task is to develop her masculine qualities: the courage to speak out, to express an idea or opinion, to create an original work, whether it be a poem, a painting, a design, or a theory, to lead a seminar, even to cast a vote! These acts all require the outwardly directed energy of the masculine. The energy of daylight, of doing and expansion; sun energy!

In dreams, the Animus is often the archetypal Guide, perhaps holding a candle or lantern to light the darkened unknown path of the dreamer. He may first show himself as a strong handsome youth, the young masculine, walking lightly beside the dreamer arm in arm, or very supportively, his strong muscled arm around her shoulder. He brings with him a sense of expectation, an excitement. The following dream snippet reflects this image perfectly.

> *I am outside of my home, the adult home of my marriage, and I begin walking out on the sidewalk in front. A young man appears; he is actually my neighbor's good-looking son, David. We exchange smiles and I feel myself blushing. He easily falls into step beside me, and we walk in comfortable silence. Then he slides his arm around my back and embraces my shoulders, pulling me against him. I feel his*

strength and his self-assurance. I breathe a sigh of relief. I no longer feel all alone.

The dreamer is a mother in her mid-thirties. Her main focus had been taking care of her three children and running an efficient household. As the children grew more independent, the woman began to take time to explore her inner life. She began reading about the Goddess and spending more time out in nature. She felt the beginning urges to pursue her own creativity.

The young man represents her young Animus, waiting for her when she ventured outside her safe haven (her house) and into the outer world. He was there for her. He gave her his support and strength. Within a short time of this dream, the woman enrolled in a computer graphics class and began working at a local herb shop. Soon after, she was creating the shop's web page and helping to design labels and brochures for a line of herbal soaps and lotions. Her new relationship to her Animus supported her venture out into the world, her expression of her creative side apart from her role as wife and mother.

Because the Animus is so integral to a woman's creative expression, it is not surprising that so many female artists, writers, Witches, and creatives are fully aware of this inner man, their cherished beloved. He is their Daimon Lover. As a woman develops her relationship to her Animus, she enhances this creative exchange of energy by opening to new and subtle ways of communion with him. In meditation, bodywork, and ritual, he may communicate with her, inspire her, advise her, and comfort her. She may have a very tangible sense of his presence in times of solitude, walking alone, or sitting in the dark quiet of evening.

In magickal workings, I will often feel the Daimon's presence gently guiding me, inspiring me in ritual, teaching me to trust my intuition and hear my own inner voice. Working magick is so much about trust, and my Daimon has taught me that.

In dreams, the Daimon/Animus may appear consistently as one figure, or constantly evolve and change along with the woman's growth. Many women dream of a particular man in their life who often is described as "strong, kind, and loving." Some women encounter him in the guise of the guy next door, while others dream of famous men: handsome actors for the more artistic or romantic Animus figures, politicians and leaders for the power- or influence-oriented Animus, spiritual figures for guides to the sacred.

If you have a consistent Animus figure emerging in your dreams, begin thinking of him in descriptive terms. What is he like? Strong, artistic, powerful, intellectual, physical, earthy, sexual, articulate, sensual, altruistic, ethical, heroic? Take a moment to write down all of his traits in your dream journal. Your answers will give you a clue as to the traits you are beginning to recognize and develop in your own self.

Here is an Animus dream from a woman in midlife:

> I am in the flush of new love, feeling all that excitement and heat. His name is Jake. He is younger than I am, a carpenter. We hold each other and gaze into each others' eyes. We talk about going to a concert to see U2 and Bono (whom I love). I begin getting dressed, pulling on a blouse and skirt. (No underwear!) We leave. Near the concert hall he pulls me into an alleyway and we make love up against the stone building. I feel as if I am conceiving a child. I am ecstatic. Jake says he needs to get the tickets, and then he's gone. I search in my purse to see if I remembered to bring my glasses. I had not. I thought, "Shit, now I won't be able to see Bono onstage." Then, just as quickly, I think, "I'll buy a pair of binoculars!"

This dream begins with the dreamer "flushed" in the heat of love. She is passionate in her relationship to this Animus. He is younger than she, a newer aspect of herself. Being a carpenter who works with his hands, we might assume he represents the more earthy, physical, and sensual side of her masculine. They talk about going to a concert. He is taking her out into the creative arena. She dresses for her adventure, leaving off her underwear; she is exposed beneath her skirt. Her sexuality and femininity are available, open. On the way they stop and make love. The dreamer is integrating this sensual masculine side; she is open and ready for it, accepting it. She feels as if she is "conceiving," beginning a new life. This is a newborn aspect of herself.

When her younger Animus goes to fetch tickets, he is significant of the masculine side of her finding the means of entry, the way in, the ability to access. U2 and Bono are symbolic of her artistic, dramatic, expressive side, her creativity. It is her young masculine that ventures to gain access to this artistic venue.

The dreamer realizes she has forgotten to bring her glasses. She won't be able to "see clearly." She cannot clarify her *artistic vision* yet. She is not able to visualize it precisely. Then she problem-solves! She'll simply buy a pair of binoculars! She knows she needs to focus her vision and acquire the tools necessary to be able to observe her Animus up close.

The Shadow Animus: Demon Lover

In many instances, a woman will choose to project her own inner masculine outward onto her partner, her boyfriend, or husband, and silently expect him to express this side *for* her. She may view him as her prince, her rescuing knight, her hero, the good provider, or the misunderstood genius. She will live her life half-full; her Animus will slumber within her. For awhile. Then she will often see him awaken with anger for being denied.

When ignored and left unexpressed, the Animus will become negative, the shadow Animus, the Demon (rather than Daimon) Lover. You will hear his voice in her tone of bitterness, her scathing sarcasm, her criticism of men, or her edgy controlling anger. This woman may suffer deep depressions or dream of a dark controlling lover, a "hit man," a vampire, a haunted lover who drains her of energy and life. Perhaps that is why vampire movies were so popular in the prefeminist conservative 1950s. Collectively, they represented the creative drain of life energy from the acres of suburban housewives. The following dream exemplifies the seductive terror of the repressed Animus.

> I am walking in a shadowy place, like the edge of a grave-
> yard. It is dark and I feel afraid. I want to find my way

home. I see a shape, a kind of dark silhouette out of the corner of my eye. I don't want to look, but I have to. It is a man, a tall dark figure in a black cloak. He looks pale, very threatening. He moves closer to me and I back away. He is evil; I feel it. He is going to kill me. His hands reach toward me. They have blood on them. "Whose blood is that?" I choke out the words. He pulls his cloak around me so I can hardly breathe in the dark. A part of me just wants to give in to him. "It is the blood of your unborn babies," he says. I wake up with my heart pounding.

This dreamer was approaching the age of fifty. A very feminine, petite woman, she was meticulous in her appearance and looked younger than her years. She had raised four children and created a comfortable home. She drove a gold-colored Mercedes, articulating the financial success of her husband's local business.

This dream frightened the dreamer and she puzzled over its meaning. The "shadowy" place where she is walking represents her venture into the unknown aspects of herself. The association with a graveyard suggests that she sees a part of herself as dead, no longer alive. Out of this dark frightening moment emerges her Animus, her denied masculine. He appears dark, as he is virtually unknown to her.

She fears him, and yet she feels an attraction to him. He is intriguing, after all. But she feels he is "evil," and will harm her. When a woman represses the expression of her Animus, he *does* become threatening. His energy turns destructive. When creativity is repressed, it turns against itself.

He is pale, without life blood, indicating that she has never "fed" or nourished him. His hands are stained with blood, the vital life force, red with passion, insinuating violence. The violence is against her own creative spirit. When she asks him whose blood it is, he first surrounds her with his cloak, blocking out light and air. She is suffocating in his oppression. He tells her it is the blood of her unborn children. This is richly symbolic of her unborn, unfulfilled creativity. His destruction has the "blood on his hands," but she herself is the murderer. By denying the expression of her masculine self, she has submerged her vital force into underground destruction. Her unborn ideas and unborn talents have died, never seeing the light of day, never reaching consciousness.

The Animus indeed has many guises. He can be a helper, a partner, a Daimon Lover who inspires us, a calm and guiding force. When ignored, he changes from Daimon to Demon, from constructive ally to destructive enemy. As Witches, we share a responsibility to our Animus, our Daimon Lover: to express his masculine energy in our creativity and focus; to bring our inner passions out into the light; to work toward balancing our intuition with insight, our feelings with understanding, our sensuality with intelligence, and our love with wisdom. The Daimon/Animus helps us to accomplish that. He is the sacred God energy of the Green Man, Herne, or Dionysos. He awaits us each night in our dreams.

Anima: Meet the Muse

Now that we have an idea of how the Animus functions within a woman's psyche, let us turn to the nature of the Anima, a man's inner soul twin. Most men are probably dreaming about their Anima on a steady basis, but they're not going to brag about it to their girlfriends and wives. Relax, gentlemen. We women understand these things. After all, we have our own Daimon Lover!

Within a man's spirit, he inherently possesses the masculine traits of focus, decision making, problem-solving, assertiveness, and rational analysis. Our culture rewards him for his efforts in his arena. However, in order to become *whole*, to have a sense of peace and inner balance, a man must eventually recognize his inner feminine, the part of himself that is capable of nurture, connection, and empathy. Jung called this inner aspect Anima, after the Latin word for "soul." She is, in a sense, the energy of the Goddess.

A man's Anima is the female part of his spirit, and she may show herself in dreams as the young maiden, the girl virgin, the love object. For poets and wordsmiths she reveals herself as Brigid, the bride, a sparkling Celtic muse. Artistic men are closer to an awareness of this inner inspiration and credit their muse with poetry and sculpture, novels and paintings. The archetypal relationship of the "artist genius" and his "beautiful young model" is not only popular myth, but haunts many studios and campus classrooms. Just ask any female art student!

Many men project their Anima onto a living woman and fantasize about making love with her. Some auto shops and garages sport calendars of nude models selling motorcycles, tools, and other merchandise. *Playboy, Penthouse,* and now the Internet provide countless images of Anima projections; perfect, silent, and willing babes who will accept anything and, in fantasy, do anything the admirer desires. The Anima then becomes merely a dream, a secret desire, an unattainable object.

In this western culture that venerates patriarchal values of power, science, and rationalism, society's collective projection of the ideal Anima appears underdeveloped, thus immature. Currently, she is expressed in our popular culture as a thin young waif, evidenced by the proliferation of young models and actresses who starve themselves into wearing a size four. I recently read an interview with a famous actress whose stated goal was to become a size zero! An appropriate symbol of how little the Goddess is valued in our popular culture.

Happily, in individual men's dreams, the Anima figure is more diverse, reflecting each man's unique taste and perception of femininity. She may appear as a dark-skinned voluptuous woman; an inviting earth Goddess, reflecting a man's sensual earthy side. She might reveal herself as a twin sister, a wife, or a beautiful movie star. Her role is to guide the man into a sense of balance, to open him to his wounded feeling function (the ability to access and express emotion, and to identify feelings), to bring him back in touch with his emotions and teach him to trust again in his fledgling intuition.

Much like the long-standing myth of the Grail, men unconsciously search for a sense of *soul,* perceiving they are somehow "missing something" in life. An Anima speaks to this unspoken longing, this intangible wistfulness; that feeling that they have been cut adrift from paradise—their lost Eden. If a man opens to his Anima, his feminine twin, she will lead him back to paradise, for her realm is his own heart.

One example of a man learning to let his Anima lead the way is depicted in the following dream.

> I am in my car, but I am not driving—my sister Morgan is driving. She has been out shopping for clothes, and now we are leaving the shopping mall. We are headed for the exit, but end up on the roof. I notice a gaping hole in the ground in front of the car, and warn Morgan about it. She ignores me and drives into it—through it, somehow—and we are moved to the other side, no problem!

The dreamer, a man in his thirties, has recognized his own feminine aspect within the guise of his sister. She, in fact, is *driving* the car. She is in control; he is letting her lead. At this point in his life he is allowing his feminine side to develop, to take the lead. He is allowing her to make some decisions about where he is headed. They are coming from a shopping trip at the mall. Shopping is indicative of opportunity, sifting through possibilities and choices, finding that which one desires to attain. She, his Anima, has been looking for clothes, symbolic of his feminine side searching for an identity, a way to express herself.

They leave the mall. The dreamer is leaving the collective, the public arena. As he exits the mainstream value system, he notices that, rather than exiting, they find themselves up "on the roof." His inner awareness of leaving the collective norm, allowing his feminine side to rise to consciousness (heading up to the "roof," the daylight) makes him a little nervous.

He notices a "gaping hole" in the ground in front of the car. Does she see it? He is feeling that allowing his feminine side, his intuition, to "take the wheel" is a bit risky. Dangers may lie ahead, holes in the supporting structure. But she breezes right on through. His feminine soul twin is able to progress, moving him into the apparent "hole" and emerging through it safely. She has surprised him by averting disaster. This could work!

Another dream that clearly illustrates an alliance with the feminine aspect is a dream reported by a musician in his mid-thirties who is married to a performance artist:

Sharyn and I are on vacation, involved in all the details of
settling in: finding a hotel, shopping for food, arranging a car,
and so on—just annoying details. Then Sharyn and I are on
a porch, the screened-in front porch of the house I grew up in.
It is night, and all manner of creatures and people are trying
to break in. A huge angry dog tries to get in by repeatedly
banging his head against the screen door. I am initially fright-
ened, but then I become angry and butt the screen door right
back to counter his efforts. He goes away. Then an unknown
person, a male, tries to break in. He shoves a large, pointed
shard of wood through the screen. Sharyn tries to shove it
back out, but I go over and grab it, yanking it away from the
intruder, saying to her, "This will make a good weapon!"
Others try to break in, but we thwart them as well.

Here the dreamer has chosen the image of his wife to be his Anima.
Ordinarily, I might suspect that in real life he projected his feminine onto his wife to carry, but the dream indicates that he sees her
not as a passive mirror for his feminine, but as a feisty fighter who is
his ally. (They are also both actively creative in their careers.)

With his feminine aspect as a partner, he is traveling to new territory; they are going on a trip, exploring a new place. The dream
begins with the dreamer arranging all the "annoying" details
involved when setting out to cover new ground. The dreamer seems
quite responsible and willing to take on preparations for this venture, as mundane as the details may be. This could indicate that he
has willingly done his homework in life, attending to life's many
demands, annoying as they sometimes are!

He then finds himself on very familiar territory—his own childhood front porch. The house is a symbol for the self; in this case, his
original self, his childhood home. A house being the structure of
the self, the front porch may symbolize the accessible front, the
façade facing the world. Perhaps the porch represents his persona,
the "face" he presents to outsiders.

The dreamer writes that "all manner of creatures and people" are
trying to break in. His soul feels attacked. Threatened, perhaps, by
the collective; perceived by him as a hostile world. The fact that

only a screen separates him from his attackers may indicate that he has no sturdier defenses in place; he feels vulnerable.

The first attacker is a brute of a dog, perhaps symbolizing a big instinctual appetite or compulsion. The dreamer uses his own anger to gather power and rebut the animal. He fights back with all his strength. The dreamer is resisting this animal drive in his life, perhaps a habit or obsession.

Then the dreamer's shadow tries to break in. The shadow represents unknown aspects in the subconscious, the denied parts of one's self. The shadow uses a sharp tool to threaten the dreamer and his wife. This pointed "shard" could be the dreamer's preferred defense: his use of sharp sarcasm and verbal barbs to wound anyone close to him.

If the dreamer does not acknowledge his use of this shadowy tool, his feminine side certainly does, for she grabs hold of it to push it away, rejecting it. The dreamer's *feelings* are aware of his barbs. He knows intuitively he ought to push it away. The ego self of the dreamer is reluctant to push the shard back, however. He comes over to claim it and reassures her, "This will make a great weapon!" He is not quite willing to give up this pointed method of defense.

A different Anima dream offered from a young man of fifteen illustrates beautifully how men search for their inner muse and long to find union with her:

> I am at home; it is night. We are celebrating my wedding. Her family is there, whom I do not know. My bride is Spanish and has long black hair; she is intelligent and deep. She actually is not wearing a wedding dress—she is wearing a long black skirt and a tee shirt. We have a lot of eye contact, love, and mutual understanding. I feel a sense of fulfillment. I go outside into the driveway to guide guests into the house, mostly her family. My bride and I walk around the party holding hands. She introduces me to all of her family.

Dreaming of weddings is a classic example of yearning for that union of soul. The divine mating of masculine and feminine. The sacred marriage of the God and Goddess. True union. The balance of yin and yang. Wholeness. Many dreamers report dreams of preparing for their wedding, choosing attire, finding their way to the ceremony.

In this dream, our young dreamer is not preparing for his wedding, he has already gotten married! He has found his soul mate bride, his muse; the inner feminine lover who inspires and offers companionship, warmth, and empathy.

Interestingly, she is Spanish; a dark-haired beauty. The dreamer is very Irish, a green-eyed strawberry blonde. His dream bride truly is his opposite, his complement. Her family represents the whole new world that will open to him as a result of this new union. He tells us that he does not know her family . . . yet. He will. There are many aspects of his new self to explore. He is a bright and sensitive young man who has a head start with his feminine guide ready in her place. With her presence, he already has access to his empathic spiritual nature, his compassion, and his creativity.

How the Anima Can Heal

The Anima can be a man's most intimate ally, his source for intuition and inspiration. She leads him into the realm of feeling and helps him to heal his wounded feeling function, which is collectively shared in our entire culture. In devaluing the feeling function, our collective society dismisses the importance of intuition, emotion, and connectedness. Our culture rejects Goddess principles.

This devaluation is what allows a corporation to make decisions that damage the environment or place the public at risk, gambling with acceptable losses for "the bottom line," placing profit before empathy.

At this point in our spiritual evolution, as this new millennium dawns, I hope to see a return of the Great Goddess and her values. I have actually witnessed a growing murmuring within people's dreams, with images of the earth, the Goddess, and the Witch emerging in dreamers' consciousness. She is returning to help us heal ourselves and our earth. If you find her in your dreams, listen and welcome her.

The Shadow Anima

Now, to complicate matters! As with women and the presence of a negative Animus, men may also experience the shadow Anima, the negative feminine within. If a man refuses to acknowledge his inner feminine and does not grow toward an integration of his masculine and feminine aspects, he may experience the ill-tempered side of the ignored feminine. She will slowly "possess" him and catch him unaware.

The negative Anima manifests herself through moodiness or a distancing preoccupation that plagues the man. He may suffer periods of depression, mood swings, and irritability, unable to express what is bothering him. He may feel restless, unfocused, and vaguely unhappy. This is the shadow Anima at work. If a man ignores his feminine side, she will rise within him and possess him jealously, through dark moods or even a catty competitiveness.

A wonderful campy example of the negative Anima was personified in the film *Fatal Attraction*, in the character of Alex, played brilliantly by Glenn Close. Alex is the outward projection of the negative Anima. At first she gets the man's attention by seduction, engaging him to live out his fantasies with her. (His character only valued her for her sexuality, as fuel for his egoist illusions.)

As he grows distant, perhaps a little bored with her and nudged away by pangs of guilt, she turns on him and exposes her worst side. She becomes possessive, jealous. "I will not be ignored!" she screams at him. She stalks him and haunts his life, becoming a peripheral threatening force that throws the male character into chaos. His marriage, his career, and his child are all threatened by Alex's unpredictability and undercurrent of violence. Her horrific act of boiling the pet rabbit is perfectly symbolic of her simmering presence in his psyche, erupting, boiling over with his worst fears. (Symbolically, rabbits are timid and fearful; prey, not predators.)

If the Anima is ignored and devalued, she has the potential to become an Alex, *within the man himself*. This movie struck a chord in the collective psyche of 1980s America, steeped in consumerism and corporate greed.

The following dream snippet reveals one man's different struggle with his rejection of his inner feminine voice.

> *I am driving my truck to work and the road gets very rough, winding and turning. I am hanging onto the wheel, but still in control. Then I hear a loud thump, a terrible sound. I've run over something, and I think, "God, I've killed a dog." I stop the truck and get out. I am walking over to this lump in the road and I see all this blood. At first, it's a deer. I see her eyes staring out at me; and then it's a woman. I've killed this woman; she's all torn up. I feel sick. I wake up in a cold sweat.*

This dreamer was in his late-thirties when he had this dream. His truck symbolizes his work and his method of how he handled things in his life. He is a strong man, determined, driven in his work, and very successful. Even when things got difficult (the bumpy winding roads), he was able to keep hold of the wheel and control his direction. He was always moving forward.

Running over the deer/woman is an excellent symbol of how "drive" can roll right over feminine values. This man was a success in his business, but at what cost? He had killed the feminine within, depicted by the gentle deer and the wounded woman. His subconscious was warning him of the high cost of his dedicated ambition.

The innate wisdom of our subconscious guides us in dreams, revealing aspects of ourselves through the people and characters who populate our dream landscape. Learn to think of these people symbolically and tune into your emotional response to them, both within the dream and in waking life, if they are familiar to you.

What does this person mean to you? What are the emotions aroused? Think about the concepts of the inner child, your internalized parents, your family system, and the Anima/Animus (as the soul twin and our unknown aspects as the shadow). Read up on symbols in the Dream Dictionary section and learn about other universal motifs. Most of all, follow your intuition and tune into your own subconscious dream language. It is the language of your soul.

3

ANIMAL DREAMS

Animals can provide the most fascinating symbolism in our dream-scape. Throughout our time on earth, humans have experienced connection, help, sustenance, gratitude, and fear in their often complicated relationship to the animal kingdom. Throughout mythology and symbolism, there are lessons learned from the animal world—insights, mirrored behavior patterns, and even spiritual guidance. Animal motifs and totems were believed to hold the power of the animal they represented, often symbolic as an emblem of protection or spiritual guardianship. It is no wonder, then, that these instinctual creatures so often show up in our dreams.

Animals as Symbols

As dream symbols, animals provide a rich tapestry of traits and behavior patterns, even personality types. When an animal reveals itself in one of your dreams, you have received a gift. On the symbolic level, first look at the mythological significance of the particular animal. There may be a parallel story and inherent lesson that will speak to your situation, or some personal meaning attached.

In indigenous cultures, certain animals were chosen by specific tribes to be their defending spirit. These animals were considered holy and powerful. Often young warriors and seekers would embark on vision quests specifically to meet and recognize their animal spirit guide. If an animal appears to you in a dream or meditative state, it may be your own spirit guide making itself known to you. If the specific animal returns in subsequent dreams, be open to its message, be expectant. As you become more proficient in your dreaming, you may actually be able to face your animal and ask it a question. A simple query might be, "What are you here to teach me?"

You may begin by looking up the individual animal in the Witch's Dream Dictionary, where I have provided many general mythic and spiritual meanings most often attached to individual animals; meanings most commonly agreed upon in North Euro-American, Anglo-Saxon, Celtic, and Native American traditions. If you enjoy a vastly different heritage, be sure that you bring your own tribal wisdom and stories into account when defining the animal's significance *for you*. Don't hesitate to research, to read other sources of information regarding your specific animal. You may have an unusual one show up in your dreamscape.

A woman in our Dream Circle had a waking dream-vision of a hyena. There were no hyenas listed in her spiritual books and resources, and she eventually worked on her own interpretation of the symbolism, paying close attention to her personal response regarding the image of the hyena. She decided that the hyena was a warning about an acquaintance, a friend who could not be trusted and, in reality, comprised a viciousness she tried to hide. We all laughed thinking about the characterization of the laughing hyena, but it made our circle member shudder. She realized her friend had a strange hollow laugh . . . and the connection and meaning were complete.

The following dream about snakes illustrates the importance of attaching our own response to an animal symbol. *Note to Freudians:* I do not subscribe to Sigmund's theory that snakes are merely phallic symbols and are always about sex. Sorry, darlings. I worship the Goddess, and to Her, snakes are ancient wisdom and rebirth!

My husband Steve and I are outside. We are on a mission: hunting snakes. He and I each carry cloth sacks. We diligently look among foliage, under bushes, rocks, and in the garden.

*As we find a snake, I hold my sack in my left hand and cap-
ture the snake with my right hand, grabbing it by its tail. Steve
quickly throws a cloth over the snake, which tames it into submission. I go around and capture more than a dozen snakes,
all a silvery-gray color. My sack is quite full. I head home, tri-
umphant. In the kitchen, I turn on the stove and heat up a
large frying pan. I pour in a generous amount of olive oil and
several cloves of fresh garlic. I then slice up the snakes on my
wooden cutting board and toss them in the garlicky oil, frying
them up!*

I had this dream a couple of years ago and was absolutely fascinated
with it upon waking. It felt very productive. In studying mythic symbols and the Goddess for so many years, my immediate association
with snakes is wisdom and rebirth. I have always felt it is unfortunate
that the Christian church downgraded the serpent to such lowly
symbology, demoting ancient wisdom into an emblem of evil and
deception.

In the dream, I am accompanied by my Animus figure; in this
instance it was my husband. Because of his "helper" role, I feel that
he is indeed a symbol for my own inner male, helping me out in the
world, in the tangled underbrush searching for snakes. This is very
close to what I actually do, researching the collective for symbology,
mythology, art, and psychology, capturing any wisdom of the Goddess I can get my hands on. In the midst of my many projects, I
often feel as if I am hunting down ideas in a jumbled cultural
thicket!

I believe that the color of the snakes, being silvery-gray, also
alludes to the feminine, as silver is associated with the moon and
intuition. So this aspect of the dream represents a search and capture quest for ancient intuitive knowledge and Goddess wisdom.

At home (the container of the self), I bring the snakes into the
kitchen, the seat of alchemy, and get the frying pan hot. Heat is
energy that transforms. By cooking the snakes I am transforming
the wisdom into a form I can absorb and digest. I am taking in this
repository of information and "cooking it up."

I season the snakes with a little olive oil and garlic. I am a cook, and at face value this is about preparation, but note that for Witches, garlic is for protection and healing. This indicates to me that in pursuing this process of alchemy, self-transformation, it requires both skill and a dash of protection.

Another side note here is that I tend to intuitively interpret knowledge in my own way, resisting formulas and recipes for learning. I am very right brained, self-taught, self-motivated, and initiatory.

I am often asked about bites in an animal dream, and have had several Dream Circle members experience snake bite dreams! If the snake bites you in a dream, this is widely interpreted as an initiation, the infliction of pain and possible death in order to initiate you into the great mysteries. This is shamanic symbolism—sharp, ancient, and specific. The message is to surrender.

Just remember that powerful symbols such as the snake may hold very different meanings for different people. There are many who are deathly afraid of serpents. If these same folks dreamt of snakes, their fear would certainly influence the symbolic meaning for them. When you dream of an animal, find the common or mythic meaning, then use your intuition and emotional response to color that meaning with your own life experience.

Animals as Wounded Aspects

Animals generally represent our nonverbal instinctual side. They reflect a time when we once lived in wildness, in closer harmony to the earth's rhythms and seasonal changes. In our current time frame, many of us feel cut off from our animal instinct, tamed into citizenship and consumerism, living and working in artificial environments. The twentieth century may have made great strides in science, medicine, and industry, but at what price? There is a restlessness and longing running like an undercurrent in our collective. Many people feel "something is missing."

What is missing is an awareness and nurturing of "soul," and a deep aspect of soul includes our animal origins, our instinct, our intuition, our interconnection with nature, from a crow's call to the voice of thunder, from a rushing stream to a turning leaf. As

Witches, we are aware of our need for soul connection in nature. It is the core of our green spirituality.

As a result of our collective mechanization, many people have dreams of wounded or dead animals. Painfully symbolic of our own wounded instinct, dreams of hurt and bleeding animals are disturbing and graphic. The following is a dream from a young woman in her early twenties.

> I am in my home, where I grew up. I walk into the kitchen. There is a scratching sound at the back screen door. I go over to the door and open it. A small kitten, bloody and crooked, tries to walk across the kitchen floor. I am almost crying looking at this poor kitten suffering. I try to pick her up and find bandages to help fix her. I tell my mother, "The kitten is broken."

The young dreamer is discovering her wounded feminine instinct. She is in her childhood home, her place of origination, in her kitchen. The kitchen is often symbolic of the seat of nurturing and transformation. Cooking food, using heat to transform, is symbolic of how we take in information, feed our souls, assimilate and change ourselves.

In this dream, our dreamer is "taking in" a small wounded kitten. Cats are associated with the feminine instinct, and the dreamer confirms this with her use of the pronoun "her." Her young instinct is obviously not developed, being a small kitten. Her descriptive word "broken" shows us that perhaps her feminine spirit was broken. The loss of blood shows the loss of vital energy, the life force. Her wounded feminine essence is bleeding, draining her of energy.

This young woman was suffering periodic bouts of depression. In the dream her subconscious is trying to reveal the source of her depression and show her that she needs to take some steps to heal herself. She needs to go find the bandages. No one else can do it. Her subconscious is beginning to alert her about her wounded feminine and urge her to take steps to bind her injury and heal.

Another fascinating dream about damaged instinct is the following dream from our Dream Circle.

I am on the street and there is an elephant—a big beautiful elephant. On top sits a terrible man, cruel. Some authority figure. He holds a whip. He is beating the elephant into submission; just beating it. It is awful. The poor elephant sinks to its knees in submission. I am horrified, crying, angry, watching this take place.

The dreamer is a woman in her thirties, beautiful, smart, and independent. This dream was very disturbing to her. We worked on the dream as a group. The elephant represents an aspect of her instinct, generous and beautiful. This instinct is being dominated by a male figure, a cruel man. I immediately thought of the symbolic word play of elephant/Heirophant. An intuitive leap. The Heirophant in tarot is a cruel judging figure, the worst aspect of the critical masculine. (This dreamer is aware of tarot, and uses it in her life.) The dominating critic was beating her instinct into submission.

Often we retain an inner critic from our early childhood, a voice berating us inside our heads, criticizing us for falling short of perfection. The Heirophant is the perfect symbol for such an inner judge—cruel, cold, and perfectionistic. The worst reflection of our internalized parent figure. Inner critics will dominate our interior life if we let them. We will always fall short if we allow them power.

At the time of this dream, the dreamer was struggling with her career choice. She was immersed in her work, respected at a high-powered, high-profile law firm, but she was beginning to question the inner price she was paying. Her more natural spiritual aspects were being dominated by her masculine strive for perfection and success. In our patriarchal culture, such commitment is valued, applauded, and rewarded. The nurturing of the soul is not.

The dreamer was very unnerved by the dream. She began to reevaluate her life and her priorities, taking more time off to be in nature, and nurturing her *whole* self, paying more attention to her sensual and instinctual needs, accepting pleasure in her life. She became more aware of her own harsh self-evaluation and began to work on softening her perfectionism.

Another example of the wounded soul, symbolized here by a raven, is revealed in the following dream:

I walk into a large building—it could have been a school or a community center. It smelled institutional, with linoleum floors and harsh lighting. I went over to a wall of lockers and opened my own. I was horrified at what I saw: a huge black crow was hanging upside down, its throat slit. Blood was draining out of the throat wound into the bottom of the locker and spilling out into the hallway. Instantly, I "knew" who had done this: my ex-husband.

Even though the dreamer had been divorced for seven years, this nightmare graphically illustrated the nature of her past relationship with her ex-husband. She begins by entering a public building; this symbolizes the collective arena. Her description of the building with its linoleum floors and harsh lighting gives us a clue as to her feelings about the collective. It isn't very welcoming. It smacks of institution, impersonal and regulated. She is wary perhaps of feeling "exposed."

Within her private locker she finds the evidence of a violent act. A crow (her magickal animal, by the way) has been killed and hung upside down. The gash to the throat indicates her wound is located in the throat chakra. Her ability to speak her truth has been savagely cut. The blood draining out of the crow is her own life force, drained by this wounding. She instinctively knows who has done this to her, and identifies her ex-husband. It is often sticky when ex-husbands and ex-boyfriends show up in dreams. Are they the Animus, soul twin? Or a symbol of the old relationship dynamic? Perhaps a little bit of both.

This dreamer is a solitary Witch who had been very private about her beliefs. She had kept them "locked away," hidden for a long time, hence the symbolic dream locker. Her first and difficult marriage had kept her from speaking her own truth; her inhibiting ex-husband had indeed "hung her up." His need for control had quietly drained her power and life force. And our dreamer had kept this wound hidden.

Now, seven years later, she was well into her new life, emerging out of her spiritual isolation, sticking her toe out of the broom closet! She was experiencing some old anxiety about exposing herself to the unforgiving collective and revealing her hidden truth.

The dreamer awoke from this nightmare disgusted and angry. The graphic depiction of the emotional violence she had once endured gave her renewed strength and determination to continue her growth and risk speaking her truth. The dreamer was me, my darlings. And rest assured, this book outs me from my little broom closet for good!

Animals as Allies

Many animal dreams are very positive, even healing. The dreamer will connect with a wise and beautiful animal and be led on a shamanic journey toward help or healing, guidance or revelation. Here we encounter the animal as ally. Here the Witch may find her helpers, her familiars, and her teachers within the dreamscape.

A dear friend of mine has dreamt of her beloved horse for years. He is tall and strong, a bit independent, and she loves him dearly. Watching them together I feel blessed to witness their silent communication and mutual love. This dreamer often dreams simply of riding her horse or gazing into his dark soulful eyes. He is her inner masculine, her instinctive power. He is her ally.

One member of our Dream Circle began a wary, tentative relationship with her own animal spirit, only to watch, astonished, as the animal developed into her powerful ally over the course of several months. It was a beautiful thing to witness. Here is her first dream, her first meeting with her future helper:

> I am at my special cabin in the woods. This is my dream cabin, my place of safety and solitude, peace and renewal. It is cozy and comfortable, with quilts and beautiful furnishings. I hear some noises outside the cabin and look out to see what is going on. There is a bear outside the cabin, pacing back and forth, trying to get in the windows, rattling the door. I am afraid. I don't want to let the bear in.

Here our dreamer is snuggled safely within her familiar warm cabin, her self-created framework. She has put this together with great care over the years; it is filled with beautiful things, comforting quilts. This is her place of refuge, symbolic of her structured safety. You might say this is her "comfort zone."

Suddenly a bear arrives at the scene. Threatening, wild, pacing, trying to get in, it tries to break through the structure, into her realm of safety. An undomesticated animal breaking into her very domesticated structure of self. She feels afraid.

In the next dream we see how her bear devises a way in:

> In a later dream, I am in an unknown house, talking with my son. (He is a young man.) He opens the front door, and suddenly three young bear cubs (one is a reddish color) come tumbling out of the fireplace. They run over to the front door and out they go.

In this dream, the dreamer is in an "unknown house," her "unknown self," possibly a new aspect of herself that is still unfamiliar to her. She is talking with her son, certainly a possible Animus figure. The inner young masculine is getting acquainted with her in this new psychic space. He opens the front door. This is the function of the Animus: He is always opening a door or showing us the way out, the way to. He is the inner masculine who wants us to grow and bring our gifts to the outside world.

When he opens the door for her, this symbolizes an opportunity. Her masculine is providing access to the world. As he provides her this chance, three young cubs come tumbling out of her fireplace. The fireplace is the hearth, the center of the home. A house is symbolic of the self, and we might assume the fireplace is the center of herself, where her own inner fire burns; her seat of alchemy and fiery emotions—desires, ambition, and passion.

The bears emerge from the ashes here, a surprise. Is something being reborn in the dreamer? Why three? Perhaps they are symbolic of the balance of three: body, mind, and spirit, reminding her to tend to all three, with equal energy.

One is reddish. Red is a fiery color, bolder than brown. He might be the feisty one of the three. The energetic cubs represent the dreamer's wilder instinctual side, newly born aspects of her growing self. They run out the front door, ready to tackle the outside world.

The dreamer is definitely going through some kind of rebirth here. From the cold ashes in the fireplace, these wonderful wild cubs tumble forth. They appreciate her inner masculine opening the door for them. They are happy to be born . . . and ready to go!

The dreamer then writes:

> My next encounter with my bear was while running in the woods. We run together in the dream; I am on all fours keeping right up with her, moving through the brush and trees. We stop to eat berries. I can taste the berries and feel the leaves on the forest floor . . . it is all very vivid.
>
> My subsequent dreams were of me actually becoming the bear, moving through woods, out in the wild. The bear does seem to come to me in times of need—when I feel like I need strength or comfort, the bear appears in my dreams. I am dreaming less and less of the bear these days, as I think I have absorbed a lot of the Mother Earth bear strength into myself.

What a transformation! From the earliest dream of her cabin in the woods, protected safely *inside* from the wild bear *outside*, our dreamer allowed the bear to give birth to cubs, emerging as her new self. Then she ran alongside the bear, sharing her path, her strength, and her berries. Our dreamer was nourished and fed by her newborn instinct, less domesticated, running out in the wild with strength and power. As she integrated the bear aspect more and more, she dreamt less of her bear helper. She has *become* the strength and power of the bear. She and the bear have merged.

The bear is a mythical symbol of great inner strength, patience, protective mother-love, and earth energy. She is associated with herbal medicine, and often appears to women who will develop her knowledge of roots and herbs, using earth medicine for healing. We now call this Dream Circle member "Bear Dreamer." She's earned it.

The next dream is of a different sort. Here the dreamer is a man in his late thirties. We see again how threatening our natural instincts can seem, and how we react in defense:

I am in a video store. Then, abruptly, I am on a trail in the mountains. Ahead of me I see two animals foraging. They are very large and look somewhat like gorillas, but with blonde hair. I "know" somehow that they are bloodsucking animals. I am a little worried, but continue on the path toward them. I watch as they turn and run into a small stone enclosure. Suddenly, they are only a few inches tall. I peek into the structure to find that they have built themselves a fire. I quickly find some stones and seal up the entrance to their hut. Then I blow out their fire.

The dreamer begins in a video store. This could perhaps indicate a sort of fantasy realm, or unreal world, as videos are, in a sense, a "living vicariously" experience. Perhaps the dreamer spends a lot of time in his own fantasy world or world of abstraction, thought, and imagination.

Then he is on a path, in the mountains. He is on his life's journey, his chosen path. He sees two large animals foraging. They appear to be gorillas, very humanlike, and they are blonde. Our dreamer is blonde, so we may assume these hairy guys are reflective of the dreamer himself. His wild and woolly side, if you will.

This is his big instinct, his wild nature. He is a little worried about facing it; approaching it seems risky. He reports that he "knows" they are bloodsucking. Perhaps he fears that his instincts have big appetites and feed on life, feed on *real* experience, symbolized by blood. They need to be fed to survive, after all. Life blood is our vital life force. Will he feed into his animal nature, or stifle it? Many men face this very question in our domesticated modern age.

As he gets closer, they turn and run for cover. His instinctual side defends itself. A stone structure. Our dreamer has walled off this wild aspect of himself. When he peeks inside, he is peeking inside himself. There he sees that the creatures are small, not threatening. They have built a fire. This is interesting. His untamed self is what keeps his inner fire going. The fire could be his creativity, his passions, the *fire in the belly*.

He quickly finds more stones and walls them in anyway, sealing their fate. They are contained, shut off. Then he blows out their fire!

I suspect a lot of men could relate to this dream. In maturing into a good citizen, a good man, many men wall themselves off from their more instinctual wild side. Their passions get locked away and the fire dies or, as in this case, gets blown out. It feels safer. This dreamer's animal instinct, which can be an ally, is now relegated to his shadow. It becomes an unknown aspect because he has walled it off. The wildness will go into his shadow and, with it, the flame of passion, creativity, and, perhaps, self-expression.

The dreamer needs to reconnect with his wildness; perhaps he needs to learn about the Green Man archetype, who reminds us each spring of the wild nature in all of us. Our patriarchal collective rewards compliance and conformity, hard work and loyalty, and many men give up the path of creativity and risk in order to live lives of safety and stability.

The Green Man archetype, Herne, the Horned One, lives in the forest; he *is* part forest, part beast. He embodies the masculine force of nature, growth, greenery, juice, and lush experience. When life feels dry and barren, structured and domesticated, spend time with the Green Man and run a little wild with him in the woods. I'm not advocating destructive behavior here, or the breaking of commitments. What I am speaking of is instinct, and allowing our animal nature to express itself.

Music, dance, drumming, and passionate lovemaking can help rekindle inner fire. Spending time out in the wild, challenging one's limits with hiking, climbing, and camping, and living away from clocks and schedules for a time can all help. Take time out periodically to live naturally; eat only when you are hungry, sleep only when you need rest, move freely when your body craves motion. Give up television, newspapers, and the Internet for two weeks. It will renew your spirit.

A teenage male dreamer reports a characteristic animal ally dream from his childhood days:

> I am walking in the dunes, in tall grasses near the ocean, toward a house on a hill. Suddenly I see a lion about twenty feet from me. He is waiting for me. I begin to run. I know to turn toward the house near the shoreline. I am running

toward the house now, and the lion is behind me, chasing me.
Then I see the lion leap out of the corner of my eye, jumping
over me to land in the grass in front of me. He sits and faces
me, looking right at me. I stop. He doesn't feel threatening to
me now. We stare at each other; there is a connection.

This is a powerful dream for the young dreamer, who remembers it
vividly, even after so many years. In the beginning we see the
dreamer venturing out into the world, exploring. He is by the
ocean, the vast expanse of his subconscious, walking in the field of
possibility. He is just beginning his life's journey.

He then sees a lion off in the near distance. It feels threatening at
first, and our dreamer turns toward the house on the hill. The house
represents his safety, his known self, which he has left to explore the
world. He runs. The lion pursues, then overtakes him, leaping in
front of him to stop and confront him. This kingly powerful beast
has stopped him in his tracks. They connect through eye contact.

As an animal ally, one could not wish for a more powerful creature. The lion is intelligent, a leader, a hunter, king of the jungle.
Our dreamer is beginning to recognize these traits in himself. He
has leadership qualities, strong ambitions. The lion is his companion, not his enemy.

If we open ourselves to our animal instincts and learn to trust
those qualities of intuition, caution, a keen sense of danger, an
awareness of opportunity, the scent of an enemy, and the clarity of
purpose, we balance our intellect and rationale. We honor our
brothers and sisters in the animal kingdom who share this fragile
earth with us. We have not survived here to dominate and destroy
our animal brothers, we have endured and thrived with their generosity, their tolerance, and their invaluable lessons about instinct.

4

THE IMPORTANCE OF SHADOW WORK

Dream work inevitably leads to shadow work. As the shadow embodies the parts of ourselves we prefer to deny or disown, often the only time we are made aware of our shadow is through dreams. The subconscious (our deeper unknown self) is very aware of our shadow, and nudges us to acknowledge it by sending us arresting images in dreams to get our attention. If we persist in ignoring these darker and unknown aspects, our subconscious will start sending us stronger and more frightening representations.

The Seeds of Denial

It is easy to see how we grow up ignoring so many aspects of our true selves. From our infant days through our childhood we are all taught to behave in a certain way. We are encouraged to display certain traits and repress others. Our personal family systems each carry their own code of *acceptable behavior*, and those who stray from that code are pressured and molded to fit in with the prevailing conformity. If one rebels, there is rejection, sometimes even punishment. These traits that we suppress, reject, or deny within ourselves become submerged into the depths of our subconscious, becoming our shadow.

Women and Shadow

As women in this culture, we are brought up in direct denial of the shadow. Little girls are "sugar and spice, and all things nice," as the old nursery rhyme teaches us. I was raised in the era of Baby Boomers, born in the mid-1950s. Through family, school, and those classic black-and-white television shows, I was taught that in order to be lovable, to be accepted, I had to be a *good* girl. I must learn to sit up straight, be polite, keep my knees together, and act like a *lady*. Girls learned at a young age that *pretty* got a lot of attention and approval, while *smart* often elicited snide comments. We were not encouraged to express a dark mood or give voice to any of those less-attractive urges. We were actually rewarded for suppressing any difficult emotion or intuitive expression. In my family, expressing anger meant getting sent to your room!

I remember, as a young girl, not knowing what to do with the darker urges of anger, rage, or jealousy that swept over me at times. I understood immediately that these emotions were simply not acceptable. Like many other girls, I learned to hide them. I also hid my visions and mystical experiences, keeping them tightly to myself. (My imaginary friend was finally discovered, however, when my mother overheard me chatting away with no one there.)

For the most part, on the outside I conformed to the standard of a nice girl, a good daughter. I accepted responsibilities, tried to be helpful, and sought approval . . . until my midteens, anyway! Then the shadow began to emerge and rebel a bit. (It was the late sixties, after all.)

Back in the fifties and early sixties, the positive fire of passion was considered unladylike, even embarrassing. I remember as a young woman feeling passionate about the ongoing war in Vietnam, and I joined in demonstrations, wrote letters, and argued fervently for empathy and peace. I was mocked for my show of enthusiasm, zeal, and optimism. I was told not to get so excited, to tone down a little and take it easy.

I made people in my family and in my high school very uncomfortable with my outward display of passion. The only opportunity for vocal enthusiasm acceptable at that time was to be a member of the cheerleading squad. To bounce and yell for your home team was acceptable; to raise your fist in slogans for peace was not. The lines were clearly drawn. You were either one of us or one of them. I ditched the melon lip gloss and Cross Your Heart Bra and joined the outcasts. It was an exhilarating time in our collective history.

Finding Our Way Back

When we begin to hide essential parts of ourselves, especially the instinctual, fiery, and passionate, we lose touch with our core energy, we lose touch with our true selves. Through dream work, women can develop a relationship to their shadow and their Daimon Lover, rekindling lost passions and seeking new modes of expression for their creative self. Ritual and magick are empowering experiences for women at any age. Reconnecting to the Goddess and her living energy both heals and inspires us. With Goddess energy women can summon the courage to become their authentic self.

The opposite of the good girl is, of course, the "bad girl." Just as approval seekers pursue positive recognition, wild girls, rebels, and "tramps" reject approval and thrive on the rush of power they feel as they repudiate the collective "norm" and stake their claim for independence. Unfortunately, the same issues of self-esteem apply, and often these "bad girls" find themselves in abusive relationships or destructive lifestyles that reinforce the spiral of low self-esteem. Addictions to alcohol, exercise, sex, or drugs are attempts to quiet spiritual pain. The spiral down is sometimes the only way through. Descent to the Dark Goddess can lead to liberation, eventually. It's just hell getting there!

Working with dreams and ritual, and finding power in the Goddess can go a long way in healing self-esteem issues and addictions to abuse. Moving from the unconscious "acting out" of destructive shadow impulses to acknowledgment and conscious choice can literally change a woman's life.

The Shadow Men Cast

For men, the collective institutes different pressures. They suffer along with us our culture's devaluation of feminine attributes. Intuition, feeling, empathy, and cooperation are suppressed and discarded so they can be seen as "real men." The cliché "big boys don't cry" is still around, my darlings.

The expectation of sacrifice and devotion to hard work for the hierarchy of status, power, materialism, and competition takes its own toll. Men are forced to sublimate their own wild impulses into the deep dark container of the shadow. They take on the archetype of the "good guy," the hard worker.

Many men seek the path of approval and pursue the acceptable archetypal roles of the Good Son, the Provider, the Soldier/Hero. These are viable choices, yes, but we must feel empathy for the lost hidden aspects these men sacrifice in order to play the part of the good citizen. The experiences of passion, instinct, creativity, and access to emotions are stuffed away in the dark along with the other less socially acceptable urges. The creative, vital, emotional force gets lost to the pressure of conformity and compliance. The Green Man goes underground.

Many men in midlife report feeling a vague sense of loss, numbness, or confusion. This is often the time to reclaim the shadow energies and spark old dwindling fires. The proverbial "midlife crisis" is the theme of many novels and films precisely because there is an underlying truth to this experience.

What is needed is dream work, ritual, and reconnection to the earth—not a new red sports car with a young babe in the passenger seat. Rather than living out the shadow destructively, men need to recognize they have the option of facing the shadow through dream work, moving toward a positive expression of their lost self, renewing their creative energy in constructive ways: with new projects, rekindling old dreams, reconnecting with the Green Man, and embracing the challenge of finding a different approach to life. It is good for the soul to shake things up now and then, not in a destructive manner that will hurt others, but in a constructive way that ignites passion and renewed interest.

Other men get caught up in playing out the rebellious archetype of the "bad boy," or Peter Pan, drifting from job to job or woman to woman, blowing paychecks on bar tabs or avoiding child support payments. They long to be free of any responsibility. For them, the reward of status and a retirement fund isn't enough. They crave freedom, but aren't exactly sure how to attain it.

Many men get caught up in the cycle of barely making it from paycheck to paycheck, doing work they despise just to get by. No heroism here, just unspoken desperation, boredom, and habitual use of television, alcohol, or drugs to numb their pain. It all distills down to the same issues: These men suffer from the same collective malady, they just express it differently. Alcohol indulgence becomes a cry for "spirit," an unrecognized need for connection, nurture, and empathy. The underlying desire is to express an authentic self.

Collectively Speaking

We all suffer the pressure to conform to society's standard. The collective drones on with its chronic influence every day in the media, in the workplace, in the pervasive pop culture itself. Through television, advertisements, radio, and movies we are constantly cued to fit in with the mundane collective. Whatever does not fit into their bigger picture gets stuffed away, denied, and discarded into shadow.

We may compress our rage and anger, our jealousy and greed, our selfishness and aggression, our sexuality and our secrets. Our wild instincts get tamed, our mystical experiences shamed. We might think, *Well . . . this is probably for the good. If we all vented feelings of rage or anger and let our "demons" loose . . . we'd have absolute chaos. Living in a civilized society requires us to conform to certain acceptable standards of behavior.*

This is basically true. In order to participate in community and cooperate with others, we all must learn to practice the art of self-restraint and respect for those around us. Exhibiting self-control shows a healthy maturity, a higher level of choice, and a deeper understanding of karma.

In addition, spiritual values such as compassion, generosity, and kindness balance our lives with a concern for soul. The Wiccan rede

"An ye harm none, do what ye will" expresses this preference for compassionate balance. The Law of Three, practiced by many in the Craft, commands proper intention and a scrupulous use of power. If we truly understand and respect power, we make a conscious choice not to use it selfishly or blindly. We regard our brothers and sisters as worthy of respect, and all living things on this earth as being connected in the same divine energy of the God and Goddess. We trust in the law of karma.

Ownership of the Shadow

However, the simple truth is that in being human and participating in the human experience, we all share in the full range of human characteristics and capabilities. An honest look at human history will reveal the depth and breadth of cruelty, violence, and greed that we humans are capable of. Individually, we like to think of ourselves as beyond the horrible stories. We psychologically distance ourselves from the persecution and torture of Witches, the Inquisition, the Holocaust, the killing fields, the lynching of African-Americans, the genocide of the indigenous American Indian people, or the mass graves in Kosovo. We would *never* do that—others do it. Some believe "evil" does it. In the Judeo-Christian and Islamic traditions, Satan (a.k.a. the Devil) does it.

As Witches, we must realize that *all* human beings share *some* impulse toward violence, greed, or jealousy. These very seeds for destructive behavior lie within our own psyche. In our growth toward integration and authenticity, we *choose* not to vent the negative energies, we decline to let the ruinous live out its full expression, we practice living our rede. We believe in karma and the law of return: That which you send out, returns to you. Yet, in our consciousness, let us not become complacent or judgmental. We must recognize that the potential for such destructive impulses lies hidden within every human heart. And we are human. In this recognition, we are humbled.

To consciously acknowledge that we have a dark and unknown side, a shadow, is to take ownership of ourselves as whole human beings; beings with yin and yang energies, dark and light, masculine and feminine, creative and destructive. To know that the entire range of emotion, action, and *all* possibility is inherent in each and every human being frees us from self-deception.

In taking such ownership, we then free others from our projections. If we deny that we have these shadow impulses, we begin to spot these very impulses in others. We project onto others the very traits we fear, suspecting these traits are deep within us, but not wanting to admit to them. We scapegoat, picking someone in the town, the class, the office, the family, the coven, to carry our shadow for us. We blame and point fingers. Often we will collectively *agree* on who the scapegoat will be.

There is an unhealthy payoff in this. We want an "other" to be bad so we can remain safe, the good one, the light one. We secretly hope that the other *will* act out our own darker aspects for us. Then we can sit innocently back, unscathed, spiritually superior, thankful that we're not like *that!* Many unhealthy marriages are based on such tacit agreements.

That is why shadow work *is* so very important. For each and every one of us who takes up this challenge of owning our own shadow, becoming aware of our whole self, accepting responsibility for our own weaknesses and darker impulses, and healing our own spirit, we take away one soul from the collective participation in shadow projection. We help to dismantle the culture's collective denial of shadow that creates the powerful need for scapegoating.

During the dark ages of Witch hunting, thousands of women and innocents were blamed and tortured, forced to carry the collectively projected shadow of the Christian church and society at that fear-filled time in history. Contagious scapegoating is what fuels the panic behind racism, sexism, and ageism. Fear feeds phobias, prejudice, and intolerance. I have always believed that ultimately, all of our choices come down to a very simple one: we can either choose *fear* or we can choose *love*. And we make this very choice every ordinary day.

To make sure such Witch hunts and holocausts never happen again, we must *all* work on owning our own shadow and taking conscious responsibility for our lives. We must all be aware of our potential for slipping into the destructive habit of self-deception, projection, and fear. As Witches, we understand all too well the consequences of ignoring this truth.

Shadow Dreams

The shadow will appear in your dreams as a mirror to your own self. If you are a woman, your shadow will be female. A sister, a friend, a coworker can all become symbolic dream aspects of your unacknowledged self. They are your reflection. The traits you respond to negatively in them are the traits you do not want to admit to in yourself. What drives you crazy about that woman in the office is that you share the very characteristic you pointedly despise. That makes you squirm in your seat just a little now, doesn't it?

In men's dreams the shadow will appear as a male. Again, a brother, coworker, friend, any masculine figure can become representative of a man's shadow, reflecting back to him his unrecognized self, some denied aspect. The dream shadow may literally appear dark, hooded, obscured. He may arrive as a thief in the night, breaking and entering into the dreamer's consciousness. (See the section on the Animus and Anima to learn how the inner masculine is an aspect of a woman's shadow and the inner feminine is an aspect of a man's shadow.)

Our dreams will show each one of us the unacknowledged aspects we need to look at. Our subconscious is interested in the truth. Our deepest self is interested in growth. Its impulse and energy moves toward truth. As we open ourselves to accept these darker denied aspects that arise in dreams, the symbols and meanings lead us toward authenticity.

The following dream shows how the shadow may also appear as a kind of monster. I had this dream when I was eighteen and at college, away from home for the first time. It was my first real shadow dream and I will never forget it:

> In my dream, I am in my room. It is dark. I see the glint off a shiny surface and move toward it. It is a mirror hung on the wall. As I look into the mirror I see my face reflected back to me. I study my face for a minute. Then it slowly begins to

change, altering into a horrible distortion. Lumps and boils begin to bulge, and I am horrified to watch as my face morphs into some grotesque creature.

I will always remember the feeling I had awaking from this nightmare. It illustrates the emerging awareness of shadow so beautifully. I, the dreamer, gaze into my reflection, my outward persona, and begin to see beyond the surface. I begin to see my "dark" side—all of the monstrous, unlovable, unknowable hidden parts of my psyche.

This dream had a profound effect on me. It actually started me on the path to study symbolism and dreams. I wanted to understand the depth of human experience and explore what lies beneath the discernible surface of things. Shadow work became a focus for my creativity and drew me into the path of knowledge. In recognizing the shadow in myself, I began to understand it in others. I began to cultivate compassion.

Another shadow encounter, this time from a male dreamer, is as follows.

I am a detective in a department store. I am assigned to the task of finding a murderer who is somewhere in the building. It's after hours, but there are still people in the store. I wander through the aisles gathering clues, and gradually, I figure out who the murderer is. I see him as he prepares to get on an escalator. I get on the escalator, too, and shoot him as he is about half way up the stairs. I ride the escalator to the top. Just as I get to the top, I see a man standing nearby, and I know instantly that he is the real murderer. I have killed the wrong man!

A compelling ending! "I have killed the wrong man." The shadow will often appear in our dreams as a dark figure, mysterious, shadowy, indistinct. He may be an intruder, a thief, a burglar. In this dream, he was a murderer. Destructive.

The dreamer was assigned to find him. His task was one of discernment: to search through the store. This represents collective opportunity, or perhaps materialism, an array of *things* that all vie for his attention. The dreamer is his ego self trying to find the shadow figure, the "murderer" within himself. What part of him was destructive? He searches for clues in the assemblage of people and things. At last he believes he has located his murderer. He shoots and kills him halfway up the escalator. Here the dreamer is under the delusion that he has identified the part of himself that he must kill. However, at the top, closer to consciousness, he "sees" the actual murderer. He has eliminated the wrong aspect of himself. His shadow survives.

We may feel reluctant to bring our shadow to light, to consciousness. He seems threatening, dark, and destructive. This dreamer obviously felt that he could identify his destructive tendency and get rid of it. When he did so, eliminating a suspected dark aspect of himself, he felt as if he had triumphed. He rose to the top of the escalator. It was then that he realized the truth: He killed the wrong man.

In trying to fit in with the collective's view of "good," abiding the rules of law and order (the police), he actually had killed off a part of himself that he shouldn't have. In other words, in his desire to be a good person he killed off an aspect of his shadow, perhaps some creatively vital instinct, only to discover that his shadow still existed in another form. When he realized he *still* had a dark side, a shadow, he was shocked and sickened that he had killed off the "wrong" part of himself.

The shadow isn't that easy to get rid of. The ego may understand the concept of the shadow, but the reality of this hidden energy can still exist, still fool us, turning up when we least expect it. Just when our intellect (ego) thinks we have it all figured out, the shadow may emerge and trip you up with a surprise appearance!

The answer lies in not trying to "wipe out" the shadow, using our ego to eliminate unwanted aspects. Sheer will or discipline cannot conquer the shadow. The answer lies in *facing* the shadow, *engaging* the shadow. Developing a relationship to it. These unknown parts of ourselves are complex and not entirely bad or dark. The shadow is rich and has many gifts to offer us. It is charged with repressed energy and full of creativity.

By turning to face the shadow and learn from it, we charm its energy, we are fed by its different point of view. By learning to hold the tension between our opposites, acknowledging the light *and* the dark, the constructive *and* the destructive, the yin *and* the yang energies, we find the middle way of balance. It is the holding of opposites that is the art to accessing our authentic self.

The Lesson of the Dragon

Think of it this way: In holding this tension of dualities, we are engaging the archetype of the Dragon. The Dragon is symbolic of *all primal energies*—the four elementals. It is earth, living in the dark cave; water, represented in its cover of fish scales; air, represented by its wings; and fire, symbolized in its fiery breath of flames. Dragon is all opposites: yin and yang, dark and light, creative and destructive. The energy of the Dragon is the perfect symbolic embodiment of how we may meet and engage our shadow. We live with the tension of our opposites. We acknowledge and respect all of our primal energies, all of the elemental forces.

Here is another shadow dream, with a twist:

> *Kate and I were in New York, traveling on the crowded sub-way. Someone in the car had a gun, a dark, shadowy guy. The police were around looking for him. They didn't find him. Kate and I had to pass through a gate, a metal detector. As we got closer to the gate, Kate pulled a gun out of her backpack. I was shocked and frightened, then angry with her. "Why the hell did you bring a gun with you?" I asked her, while thinking, Now we will be held up and detained, maybe even arrested. Then I looked over at her and saw the gun change. It was decorated beautifully like a sacred pipe, with beadwork and feathers.*

In this dream, the dreamer, a woman artist in her midforties, trav-els with her shadow; her companion Kate is her ally. As we acknowledge our shadow and integrate it, our unknown self becomes our ally. This can happen at midlife as women move toward self-acceptance and integrate the masculine aspect into their awareness.

The dreamer and her shadow are in the thick of the collective: a big city subway, subterranean, the realm of the shared subconscious. The subway itself is a perfect symbol for the undercurrents in the collective—the hidden energies that flow through society like an underground stream.

A masculine shadow figure threatens the collective. There are many expressions of male rage and violent undercurrents moving in society at this turn of the millennium. Men are collectively suffering from a wounded feeling function, and this, in turn, affects all of us. The police (collective law and order) are trying to locate the threatening male figure, perhaps the symbol for underlying male anger. Men suffer from the restraints of the collective as much as women do. Here, the law, rules, and regulations cannot "correct" the problem of men feeling disenfranchised. This dark side of the collective masculine will not be healed through police work. It will be healed in recognizing the collective wound to feminine values and men's feeling function. "Men with guns" symbolize man's desire for change; they want it now—their collective anger craves immediate impact.

Next in the dream, the two women have to pass through a gate. People are collectively funneled through this gate; perhaps symbolizing a rite of passage. This may signify the gateway to menopause, as this dreamer is at the appropriate age to feel pressure in approaching this impending change of life.

The metal detectors will obviously find hidden weapons. The dreamer glances at her friend, her shadow. Her shadow has brought a hidden weapon, a gun! Her shadow has endangered them, perhaps detaining them by packing a gun—a weapon of change by force. Our dreamer feels anger at her shadow: Why has this aspect done this to her? To expose her to possible detainment? What aspect of her shadow is "holding her back"? Perhaps fear, if the gun was packed for protection. Or, maybe she feels that time itself is running out; she is *under the gun* at midlife?

Next, the gun turns into a beautiful sacred pipe. The weapon, an instrument for change and destruction, has transformed into the pipe, an instrument of peace and prayer. Her shadow is a Trickster. She has brought along the means of change and transformed it from a deadly weapon to something sacred and beautiful.

This is an engaging dream, complex with undercurrents of the shadow within our masculine collective, and the workings of shadow within the dreamer. The collective masculine is suffering and angry. The empathic dreamer feels this. Her own shadow has become her ally, and here plays the archetypal Trickster. Transformation takes place at the gate—the passage to a new life, menopause, the next phase of her life journey.

Women in Native American tribes are not encouraged to become Medicine Women until they have passed through the rite of menopause. Only when a woman stops her monthly moon and retains her powerful "wise blood" can she gather and keep the power needed to become a Medicine Woman.

The dreamer is shown by her shadow, the Trickster, that the impact of menopause *will* be sacred. She will be able to retain her power and use it for spiritual healing. She will become the Crone, the Witch, the Wise Woman. This is a difficult phase for women in this youth revering culture, and the dreamer is aware of her fears, but also of her inner strength.

Accepting Our Shadow

In accepting our shadow as an ally, we free up the energy we waste on repressing it. This is not about letting the shadow run wild. I am not encouraging an "acting out" of shadow impulses. In truth, one sees the dark side of the destructive shadow erupt *unconsciously* in individuals who ignore the existence of shadow and refuse to undertake the task of shadow work.

By *denying* the presence of shadow, acting all "sweetness and light," we become unwitting players in the shadow's drama, for it will gather energy underground and suddenly loom large, startling us with its dark energy. It may trickle out in a scathing remark or a jealous lie whispered in pettiness. It may overtake us with an unexpected spike of rage that we feel compelled to vent, not knowing why. Ignorance, then, is not bliss, but merely unconscious behavior.

It is imperative that we acknowledge our shadow, understand it, and work with it. Humor helps. When you feel the shadow slip out in a cutting remark or pang of envy, make fun of it. Humor defuses the power of the shadow. That's why dark humor and black comedy feel so therapeutic—laughing at our darker selves is healing. Laughter at the shadow can charm its energy from destructive to creative.

What I am encouraging here is self-acceptance and humility. An awakening to the fact that "there but for grace, go I." In embracing our whole self, we free up tremendous amounts of energy once wasted in repression and denial. It takes mammoth quantities of effort to construct the wall of denial; to build the illusion of perfection; to be only Glenda the Good Witch, perfect and golden.

Besides, perfection is overrated. You can quote me on this. None of us are perfect, darlings, so just relax. And when you're tempted to turn your ex into a toad, call up a friend and have margaritas instead.

Working with the shadow in dream work, then, becomes an important task. In order to clearly inform our magick and free the flow of power, we must be clear in our self-awareness. Unacknowledged shadow aspects can cloud our thinking and negate energy flow. Unconscious desire for power or manipulation over others will color your work with a destructive edge. So look at your shadow dreams with an unwavering eye and a clear mind.

Ask yourself:
What are my shadow characteristics?
What are my unconscious motivations?
Of what am I ashamed?
What hidden secret do I fear?

Dream work takes courage and commitment to growth. The Witches' path is ever-turning, drawing one deeper into the mysteries and truth of the universe. In looking within, we are seeking no less than wisdom itself. For Witches know better than anyone that the truth lies within your own heart. If you cannot find it there, you will not find it elsewhere.

5

Nightmares and Night Terrors

When we block expression of our shadow—our unknown, unacknowledged self—we cut ourselves off from a fundamental source of energy that burns with truth. We suffer because the construction of denial and defense that we create to shield our ego selves requires tremendous energy to remain in place. Imagine an inner army of immense strength whose sole purpose is to keep our illusions in position, to keep the status quo, to keep the facade of denial in place, like a lid on a boiling pot. This is an enormous waste of our vital self, our essential energy. It's exhausting.

When our subconscious realm reaches a boiling point, it bubbles over, erupting with nightmares and startling dream images in order to get our conscious attention. If we continue to ignore the warnings and messages in these frightening dreams, we may then suffer depression, neurosis, and anxiety. But if we can welcome these messages and understand that our subconscious mind is using its dynamic energy to break through our walls of containment, we discover that nightmares and disturbing dream images can be a powerful force for healing, for integrating the truth. A push toward consciousness.

The following nightmare illustrates the power of our subconscious mind to wake us up from our sleep of denial and pay attention.

I am having a quarrel with a young man. I am younger in the dream, perhaps in my late twenties. Suddenly, we have resolved the argument and are climbing into bed. When he lies down on his back, I see that his stomach is covered with blood. The blood is thick and clotted. I wake up in horror.

The dreamer is a soft-spoken man in his late thirties. In his dream he is arguing with a young man who represents his own shadow side. He is fighting with his shadow, his unknown self, uneasy with it. Then the argument (conflict) is over. He has resolved his struggle for now. They climb into the same bed, which symbolizes the acceptance of their mutual relationship. Our dreamer has made peace with his shadow. But at what price? He notices the blood. His unknown self is wounded, right in the abdomen, the seat of emotion, "gut feelings," intuition, vulnerability. This tells us that the dreamer has suffered a wound to his ability to honor his gut feelings, his instincts. By arguing with his shadow side and winning with his intellect, he has sacrificed his ability to access his feelings. The congealed blood symbolizes the blocking of his vital life force. His center of emotion and instinct is clotted, damaged. The coagulated dark blood tells us this is an old wound.

Many men in our collective have been wounded in their feeling function, their intuition. In a culture that celebrates physical power, "manifest destiny," status, and technology, the feminine values of intuition and emotional intelligence are cast aside. Men often feel this wound in their gut. It is a vague sense of loss that is difficult to face and come to terms with. There is little support in our culture to help a man get back in touch with this lost feeling function. Dream work helps, as well as ritual and magick, and, perhaps most importantly, the recognition and inclusion of the Goddess into their life. The honoring of intuition, dreams, and sensuality. See the section on the Anima for more insight into wounded men.

Often a nightmare can be an awareness of a collective wound or communal affliction. The next dream reveals startling imagery to depict a collective truth:

I am in a large building, like a college lecture hall or a civic center. I feel compelled to open this big heavy door and walk into the auditorium. The light is dim at first, and I am aware of a presence in there, but do not see anything clearly at first. As my vision adjusts I notice that are dozens of bodies on the floor. Strewn everywhere. They are women. As I walk closer I see that they are all beautiful models. They turn their heads toward me, their eyes are staring at me. It is then I really see what is happening: their hands have been cut off and their legs have been chopped at the knees! They are all still alive, but just lying there. The most horrible thing is that they cannot speak. They all lie there with their mouths opening and closing like fish, with no sound coming out. They are mute. And the overall picture is so horrifying, so terrible, that I wake up.

This is another one of my own dreams, a nightmare that so eloquently revealed how the collective's view of beauty and femininity wounds women. The public building and lecture hall reveal the collective nature of the setting. The sense of it possibly being a college gives me a clue that this is "educational." This message is being taught, being learned in the collective mind. I enter into the hall through a heavy door. In my own life, I usually find myself living on the outside of the collective; the heavy door separates me from what is inside. (Perhaps the heavy door is denial.)

Once within the collective hall my vision adjusts and I am slowly able to see more clearly. My perception of this truth is becoming clearer, sharpening in focus. The women all represent the collective's ideal projection of femininity. They are models, our culture's epitome of female beauty. The totality of "perfection." These models, these symbols of beauty, are wounded. They are missing their hands.

Our culture's ideal of femininity has made women handless, unable to grasp, to make, to create, to care for, to touch, to *do*. We have been cut off from our ability to contribute. The models are also cut off at the knees. This, too, informs us of how the narrow projection of womanhood has collectively "cut women off at the knees." Women feel powerless.

Another disturbing aspect of the dream was the women's inability to speak. Their mouths move like fish, but they have no voice. No sound emerges. They are mute. When woman are constrained to a projection of false femininity, they are unable to express themselves, to communicate, to speak the truth. They feel as if they have no voice.

Thankfully, there is a solution. With the return of Goddess spirituality, bringing a needed balance to the once strictly male view of spirit, we will collectively adjust our values of what constitutes real femininity. The rise of Wicca and Craft, neopaganism and Druidry, will help to heal the wounds of our two-thousand-year-old reign of patriarchal values. It won't happen overnight, but the collective pool is changed by each ripple we create.

Interestingly, the following nightmare was experienced by my husband during the same time period as the previous model dream:

> A middle-aged blonde woman is preparing to address a crowd in an auditorium. There is a commotion of some sort, and she appears, in the rear of the auditorium, impaled on a number of spikes within a bizarre shrine. As soon as I become aware of her there, I realize this is the second murder of this kind.

The auditorium is a clue of the collective nature of this dream, being a public arena. The woman will be addressing the crowd. She is middle-aged and blonde, so we may assume she is representative of my husband's Anima (as he is also middle-aged and blonde). She symbolizes his feminine twin, getting ready to face the collective and speak. Before she gets her chance to express herself she is murdered, impaled by spikes. This is a terrifying image, violent and almost ritualistic. The dreamer feels his inner feminine will be murdered, killed in the collective arena.

He is all too aware that the culture rejects feminine values. The mention of the "bizarre shrine" reflects the dreamer's awareness that our collective kills femininity, and that this act of death is worshipped in this culture. Her death is a ritual, perhaps even symbolic of the Death of the Goddess, revealed to the collective crowd as a shrine to the truth of what they "worship." The dreamer is aware that this is "the second murder of this kind." As he explained to me, "This wasn't the first, and it wouldn't be the last."

On a personal level, my husband felt that the dream represented his own struggle with honoring the feminine in his life. He fed his creative self and expressed his emotional life by painting, yet still wrestled with the way his work was often misunderstood, misrepresented, and treated as commodity in the "public" arena. (He is very successful and sells his paintings quickly.) Perhaps he feels conflict over the pressure of success. The dilemma an artist faces in success is the temptation to repeat oneself. Galleries will often pressure artists to simply keep repainting, recreating what sells . . . certainly the death of creativity! Here symbolized by the death of the Anima.

The following nightmare was recently told to me by a shy, attractive sixteen-year-old woman. Touching also upon the collective's view of beauty, as well as facing the inner shadow, I suspect that many young women can relate to her dream:

> I am watching television in my dream, at home, at night. I am watching a "preview" for a horror movie. In the preview a woman is sitting at a vanity, looking at herself in the mirror. There are waves of some kind of energy around her, not coming from her, but going into her. It was scary. She gets up and starts to walk around the house, going down hallways and checking behind doors. As she walks away from each door, it kind of opens by itself a little. This feels really scary. Then I am in the dream; I am the woman in the preview. I am suddenly outside, and it is dark. I am in a scary neighborhood. There is a girl my age following me. She comes up to me and moves around to my side, touching me on the shoulder. It's confusing. I don't know her. She walks away. My boyfriend is there now. And the girl again. My skin starts to whither and wrinkle, like a mummy. It's terrible. The girl says to me, "You are ashamed of your body, that's why." She is trying to teach me a lesson or something. I think it's about hating myself. My boyfriend says (referring to the girl), "She's been using me. It's killing me." And he starts to look bad, and I get really scared and try to scream, and this wakes me up.

As the dream begins, our dreamer is watching television; she is not participating in life, but watching a "preview." Perhaps this reflects her age, her sense that she is not yet allowed to fully participate in "life," but can only look at a preview of what may lie ahead. It also may indicate a preference to fantasy or living vicariously through watching others, not risking her own involvement.

She is watching a woman looking into a mirror. There is a double layer of meaning here: The dreamer looks at the television screen, a kind of "mirror" of society, of life, as the actress looks into her mirror at her vanity. Both women are self-reflective. Both are "looking into their vanity," their concern for appearances.

The actress has rays of energy entering into her, and the dreamer finds this scary. Perhaps this represents the electronic "input" of collective power, the influence and force of the media on how we perceive ourselves. Is the collective feeding into her fear?

The woman rises and begins to explore hallways and open doors. This is about investigating options and opportunities. Our dreamer is seeing herself in the actress and wondering about the different opportunities, various choices she will have. What door will she open in her life? And where will it lead? Our dreamer has fears about this. The unknown lies on the other side of each door.

Then the dreamer enters the "preview." Her identification with the actress is complete. She has entered her world. (The actress has been an aspect of the dreamer all along, and now the dreamer has joined her aspect.) She finds herself in an unfamiliar "scary neighborhood," at night. This represents unknown territory and exploring the dark unconscious. Our dreamer is struggling with this territory; it frightens her to explore it. This is shadow territory, facing the unknown and unacknowledged self.

Her shadow, a girl her own age, comes up to her from behind. The dreamer is unaware of her shadow; it has snuck up on her. She feels confused, not recognizing the girl as herself. She is not quite ready to face her own shadow side.

Her boyfriend shows up, then the shadow girl again. The boyfriend is her projected masculine, her Animus, as yet unknown and undeveloped. (He is out there in the dark with her.) He signifies her masculine attributes that are presently hidden from her. Their relationship is symbiotic and unconscious. As the dreamer begins to suffer, watching her skin whither like a mummy's, the boyfriend suffers as well. Her whole self is suffering.

The shadow tries to tell her a truth: "You are ashamed of your body." The dreamer realizes this is some kind of lesson. Perhaps the dreamer fears aging, signified by the wrinkling skin, and fears that as she faces adulthood, her aging will make her less attractive. She fears she will be mummified, dead, preserved, dry. Her spirit is anguished here. There is no flowing water of life in this dream, there is only darkness and dryness.

Her boyfriend tells her that the shadow has been "using him." The dreamer's shadow manipulates her Animus, her unknown masculine, and it's killing him. She is destroying the male aspect within her; he cannot come to life. She is holding him back, perhaps by accepting a distorted view of her own femininity (the actress searching the vanity mirror for validation). Her helper, her Animus, cannot survive in this realm, there is no place for him.

She will not grow unless she faces responsibility for her own shadow and comes to terms with her perception of beauty and how she feels about her body. She has a struggle ahead. She must fight the collective that is feeding into her inner fears and find her own reality, beyond the world of television, beyond the world of her dark dread. She must look at herself and find her own power within, in the form of her inner masculine.

If the dreamer is able to create a relationship to her inner male guide, her Daimon Lover, and allow him to flourish, he will take her by the hand and lead her to balance. His gifts will be strength and courage. This dreamer happens to be on the Wiccan path, so she will have resources available to her. If she can open herself to the lessons of the Goddess and God and do her "homework," she will be fine.

When a nightmare jolts you awake in a panic, cold sweat covering your body, your heart pumping wildly in your chest, pay attention. There is an important message here. Spend time with your nightmarish images, as awful as they might be. Familiarize yourself with the symbols in the Witch's Dream Dictionary and write down your nightmare and the associations your intuition guides you toward. Most of all, remember, many gifts come wrapped in strange packages!

6

Beginning Your Dream Work

In beginning the process of dream work, always operate intuitively. Follow hunches and feelings. Allow your emotions to surface as you study your dream images. Let your intuition and feelings guide you to associations and correspondences. Follow the leads given to you in the Witch's Dream Dictionary, and make note of your own symbolic meanings in your own personal dream dictionary and dream journal.

A Dream Worksheet

Here is a dream worksheet to get you started. Remember, nothing is written in stone, so begin where you feel most comfortable. Use these suggestions as a guide for exploration. If you are starting your own Dream Circle, use this worksheet as a model to explore each members' dream. You might choose to have each person take turns asking questions and facilitating the discussion.

Relax

To begin your dream interpretation, take a deep breath and relax. If you are able to quiet your mind into a receptive alpha state, you will be more open to intuition and the nonverbal language of symbols. Light a lavender candle if it helps you to let go of the mundane world.

MAKE NOTE OF YOUR DREAMSCAPE

What was the environment? Were you inside or outside? Exploring your inner self, or your outward choices? If you are in an interior space, a house or building, chances are you are exploring your "sense of self." If the space is public, such as a school or auditorium, the psychic space you are exploring is the collective, the arena of peers, outside influences. If the space is your office or workplace, the dream may be about your job, your career. If you are outside, you are exploring your world—where you are in life, your destiny, your journey, your progress. Perhaps you are "covering new ground" or "exploring new territory," indicated by traveling to a foreign country or unfamiliar landscape. What is the season, the weather? This will give you a clue as to the *context* of the dream. The weather may symbolize the season of your emotional growth, the quality of your inner experience. Winter would indicate a different emotional state than summer, for instance. Winter is cold, frozen, and static. Spring is new beginnings, rebirth. Summer is expansive, warm, and lush with growth. Autumn may indicate a bittersweet time of letting go and turning inward. Stormy weather can indicate emotional turbulence.

MOVEMENT

Next, take notice of how you are *moving* in your dream. Are you walking, climbing, running, swimming, driving? Each way of moving in the inner world is a clue to the *nature* of your dream journey. Are you solo, or with others?

DESCRIBE MOVEMENT

Make note of *how* you were moving: quickly, excitedly, or slowly struggling. Perhaps you were dancing seductively or running in a panic. Pay attention to how you feel about your body in the dream. Are you tense and tight? Or are you able to run free and unencumbered? Is this how you usually move? Once you describe your movement, clue in to the *emotion* you were feeling as you moved. Were you feeling frustrated, scared, exhilarated, apprehensive? Mark down this feeling in your dream journal.

FIND YOUR THEME

What was the theme of your dream? Oftentimes, we may detect a theme running through our nightly reveries. We may have a series of dreams about work, goals, family issues, personal growth, love and desire, facing the shadow, or integrating our twin, our Anima or Animus. Subthemes, such as striving for recognition, struggling upward (for spiritual progress), feeling unsupported, exploring new territory, or giving birth to a new aspect, are all commonly shared dream experiences. Was it a dream of revelation, or a dream of healing? Was your subconscious forcing you to face something in yourself that you were denying? Follow your feelings to discover your own dream themes and make note of them. If it is unclear to you at first, begin writing down the very basics. For example: career or identity issues, family, running away from, searching for, meeting a lover. After awhile you'll begin to detect a pattern of intent.

USE DREAM CONCEPTS

Familiarize yourself with the definitions of archetype, Anima, Animus, shadow, and collective (all were explained previously and are listed in the Witch's Dream Dictionary). Begin by recognizing these concepts within your dream story. Read about how they function in our subconscious, and discuss with others how these elements function in your dreams. Spotting your shadow or recognizing your Animus will become second nature after you acquaint yourself with these conceptions.

WORK WITH DETAILS

After you are comfortable with the climate of your dreamscape and understand the overall theme of what you were experiencing, begin to notice the smaller details. In doing this, we move from the big picture to specifics. Colors, animals, parts of the body (body parts correspond to chakras), elements, and symbolic objects all have meaning. Use the Witch's Dream Dictionary to help jump-start your understanding of symbols. Look up correspondences in appendix A. See what clicks!

Detach Yourself

Finally, after you have laid out your dream symbolically, step back from it and try to view it as a myth or story. Even a movie. If you can draw back from it enough to detach from it briefly, you will have a little more distance from which to focus in on the meaning and use your intuition. This is your own mythic story, and you are the lead.

Use the Witch's Dream Tools

Utilize the information in chapter 7, A Witch's Dream Tools, and try Association or Active Imagination. Talk it over with a friend or, ideally, a Dream Circle. You will begin to understand your symbolic language the more you play with it, read about it, and work with it in your dreams and dream journal. It takes practice. Sometimes even the most seasoned interpreter may get completely stumped by a particular dream. When that happens, just let it go. You will find that somehow, somewhere, you will be given a clue to its true meaning. Perhaps within a book you pick up or a synchronistic conversation with a friend, you will suddenly discover a meaning you had not thought of. (Read the entry for *moss* in the Witch's Dream Dictionary for an example of how this happened to me!) Often, a second related dream will be offered up to you from your subconscious in an attempt to clarify the puzzling one. Set your intention before you fall asleep, asking your inner guide to help you understand your dream. Help is always available to the Witch, after all. We need only ask for it!

A Sample Interpretation

To illustrate how to begin thinking in symbolic terms, here is a sample dream from our Dream Circle and the process used in its interpretation.

> *I am walking up a trail, making my way easily. The terrain becomes a little more difficult and I have to contend with rocks and stones and a sharp incline. I start to slip a little on the loose dirt and small rocks, and struggle to hold my footing. Then I look down and see my feet. I am wearing soft rubbery pink sandals . . . like those jelly sandals. I am pissed. "I'm wearing the wrong fucking shoes!" I yell in disgust.*

We all shared a big laugh over the punchline in this dream, each one of us recognizing that universal moment in life when we realize we're not prepared. First note that the dreamer is outside. Her environment is a path, a mountain trail. That tells us that the dream is about her progress, her chosen path. It is a solitary one, as she is alone on the trail, "off the beaten path," apart from the collective mainstream. This journey is personal. Because her movement is upward, we may assume it reflects her spiritual progress, her aspirations. As her path becomes more difficult, we see she is encountering some minor obstacles, represented by the stones and some slippery conditions. We see she perseveres. The slope goes up sharply. This shows her progress is entering a critical phase, a difficult passage. She glances down to her feet. Her footing is her support, how firmly she stands. She is aghast. She has on absurd shoes. We might assume from the pink color and her own description of jelly sandals that she feels unprepared for the rough terrain of her ascent. These shoes may represent her past choices and how well she has prepared for her trek, her path upward.

Remember the saying, "To truly know a person, walk a mile in their shoes"? In looking down at her shoes, which are an aspect of her choices, her identity, we see that she is reevaluating her choice. She realizes that she has not chosen the "right" shoes for her journey. Perhaps she feels unprepared for the difficulties she is facing in her progress. Or perhaps she now feels it is time for a change in her life. That in order to continue onward and upward, she needs stronger, more rugged "shoes" to support her. Maybe the shoes represent her spiritual tools, her means to progress and move forward. Her support system.

To briefly wrap it up, the dreamscape was an outdoor trail. This shows what the dream is concerned with: the dreamer's individual path in life. Her movement tells us that she is walking, progressing upward, then slipping a little and trying to get a firmer foothold. Her theme would then be: her progress in life, perhaps spiritual, on her chosen path. Conceptually, she is alone here, so there are no confrontations with shadow or masculine Animus figures to guide her.

The path is off from the collective, so we know this is all about her own choices. The details, of course, are the pink jelly sandals. In using some tools of intuition and association, the dreamer remembered that she once wore a similar pair of pale pink jelly sandals twenty years ago back in college. Suddenly she felt that her dream was telling her that in order for her to progress, she had to make some new choices, leaving behind some of her old belief system from her younger days. She had outgrown her earlier expectations that were now limiting and restricting her growth. She felt she was, at midlife, going through a total reevaluation of her deeply held values and discarding the old that no longer supported her in where she was headed.

Starting a Dream Journal

Choosing a dream journal is a very personal matter. Some dreamers may favor a blank white page, feeling that lines only interfere with their rapid recording of dream images, while others select lined paper to precisely contain their thoughts and dream impressions. The size of the journal is everything; a dreamer should take size and format into consideration when selecting a journal. Choose one that feels comfortable in your hands. If you decide to keep your journal at your bedside, which I recommend, select a size and format befitting your space.

The women in my Dream Circle use everything from small hardbound journals to school-sized, three-ring binders, complete with subject tabs for sorting dreams by theme! Not everyone approaches dream journaling so methodically. One woman in the circle simply uses a lined yellow legal pad. The choice is yours. Just keep in mind that your journal must feel inviting to you. Select a blank book or notebook that is appealing to your sensibilities and reflects your personality. The care with which you choose this simple tool will inform your subconscious that you are serious about listening to your dreams, that you are prepared to accept the information and insight that dreams tender. As with any working of intent, your care in preparation and attention to detail will only enhance the energy and power of your dream work.

One option is to make and bind your own journal with handmade papers and ribbon, available in art and craft stores. You can also create your own cover on a notebook by pasting a favorite photograph or painting, even a post card image that captures your imagination and speaks to you.

As you work in your dream journal, don't hesitate to add pictures, cut outs from magazines, lines of poetry, even pressed flowers and herbs. Often upon waking with a striking image still in my head, I will be aware throughout the day of how the image is repeated and reflected back to me. Synchronistically, I will hear a song lyric, or open a magazine and see an image that spoke to me in a dream the night before.

In a recent dream I had, I was holding a vibrant glowing baby who smiled up at me and spoke eloquently! The next day as I opened the mail, a colorful advertisement fell from a bill envelope and caught my attention. It pictured the radiant beaming face of a beautiful baby, so very much like the divine Wonder Baby in my dream, that I cut it out and tacked it up on my computer to remind me of my dreaming sense of wonderment. I felt the baby symbolized the conception of a new project being born, and it filled me with confidence to gaze at the bright lovely face of this merry little infant, confirming birth of new creativity.

Think of your dream journal as a work-in-progress. In it you will be writing down your dreams and snippets of ideas about their meanings, collecting impressions and images. Use colored inks and highlighting pens to emphasize words or celebrate insights. Paste star stickers and cut out pictures if you like, to add energy and magick to special dreams that reflect your growth or connect you with an archetype or myth. Over time, looking back through your journal will fill you with amazement, even awe, at the wisdom and complexity of your own dream language and personal epic. This is your mythic journey!

Putting Pen to Paper

As you begin the process of dream interpretation and journaling, take a deep breath and remember that perfection is overrated! Don't even waste a minute worrying about your handwriting or your spelling or capturing the right words to describe your dream. Just write. Let it flow. Don't worry about it making sense, and resist the urge to shape it with more rational language. The subconscious mind is rich in its layers of complexity, and it will send up symbols, images, and words that may have multiple or layered meanings to you. These words are personal flags. Write them down freely. Don't censor. Simply write. Get it all down as soon as you as you wake up. Yes, darlings, *especially* before that first cup of coffee. If you wait until you are more alert and into your waking state of mind, you may lose important pieces of the dream.

Casting a Dream Spell

Once you begin your dream journal, place it near your bedside with a favorite pen or pencil next to it. One woman in our Dream Circle also positions a small pen-sized flashlight nearby for midnight dream recording!

Setting your intention as you prepare for sleep helps to inform your subconscious that you are receptive to dream images. Create a nightly ritual for yourself that centers you and opens your mind for dreaming. If you are pondering a decision in your life or seeking an answer for a problem facing you, quietly meditate on your question for a few moments before going to sleep. Ask your inner self to show you an answer in your dreams. As you discover your personal animal guide, or spirit guide, you may ask them to reveal an answer to you. Invite them to visit you in dreamtime and speak to you. This may sound a bit New Agey, but it really does work!

Try lighting a light blue votive candle in the evening as you prepare for bed, take a bath, or read with a cup of tea. (Just don't fall asleep with the candle lit, please!)

Sipping tea with star anise, nutmeg, and cinnamon is said to enhance psychic awareness. Burning cedarwood incense is thought to invite dreams.

Lavender, jasmine, and orange oils enhance relaxation and dreaming. Indulge in a warm bath before retiring, adding ten drops of jasmine oil, five drops of lavender, and five drops of orange to the bath water. Get into the tub, and anoint a light blue candle with these oils as you ask your inner self to remember your dreams. Breathe deeply, relax, and anoint your temples and third eye (the center of your forehead just above your brows) with lavender and jasmine. *Note:* Please use essential oils with caution, especially if you are pregnant or have skin sensitivities. Always consult a professional aromatherapist before using any oils other than lavender or tea tree oil.

If you do not have jasmine oil, try inhaling the sweet scent of honeysuckle for complementing your psychic awareness. The scents of blooming narcissus and mimosa are also purported to bring dreams and inner awareness.

To make an easy Dream Pillow Sachet, take a clean, fancy napkin or hankerchief (I often find lovely lace-trimmed napkins at thrift stores and flea markets) and place a cotton ball in the middle. Add a drop or two of lavender, jasmine, or honeysuckle oil. Add a few pinches of lavender buds and lemon balm leaves. Toss in a couple of rose petals. Bundle up your herbs and tie the hankie with a blue or lavender satin ribbon. Keep these sachets tucked in your bed linens and under your pillows, even in your pajama drawer. Their sweet scent will enhance your sleep and welcome dreams.

Sleep on sky blue sheets or even a light blue pillowcase to help amplify your dreaming mind. Remember that all of these implements merely help to focus your will and intention to open your mind and dream. It is ultimately up to you and the power of your intent to create the spell you need to center yourself and remember your dreams. Your subconscious will reward your dedication.

Creating Your Dream Dictionary

As you begin recording your dreams in your personal dream journal, you will be ready to compose your own dream dictionary. Don't worry, you'll start slowly, and with every new dream you will find new symbols to add. It will be an ongoing process, alongside the dream journal itself. You may choose to use the same notebook, or blank book, that you record your dreams in. Or you may choose to begin a separate notebook for your dictionary of symbols. How you approach your organization is up to you and your personality.

I often scribble my interpretive words in the margins alongside my written dreams, highlighting important words or adding insights. This makes for a rather messy and jumbled journal, but it suits my personal intuitive approach.

In our Dream Circle, members have very individual approaches to their dictionaries. One very organized woman has a separate dictionary section, completely alphabetized, that she updates periodically. Others have recorded their symbols on blank pages, organizing them loosely into favorite categories such as: Animals, Family Stuff, Anxiety, Passages, and so on. The most important aspect of creating your Dream Dictionary is that it is uniquely yours, reflecting your own supply of meanings and interpretations.

In interpreting dreams, I have found that all dreamers have their own particular perspective, colored by their personal history of experiences and their emotional responses to life encounters. Meanings can be projected onto objects that are highly personal, based on childhood memories, fears, or attachments. That is why it is often so frustrating to pick up a copy of a published dream dictionary promising "Thousands of Dreams Interpreted" only to find no resonance with what is written, no connection to our individual truth.

There are, indeed, many symbols that we do collectively share as human beings, yet even deep-seated universal symbols such as a "snake," for instance, can mean different things to different dreamers, depending upon the emotional response to the snake (fear? awe? fascination?).

One woman might find that dreaming of a bear speaks to her about her deep inner wildness, her powerful untamed instinctual side. And a different dreamer may feel that the bear is symbolizing his need to hibernate, go within, and find solitude.

The important thing to remember in dream work is this aspect of individuality. Study the meanings ascribed to your particular symbol and examine your own personal response, filtering the meaning through your own intuition and emotional reaction. You might choose to record your symbol with both your own personalized meaning and the broader collective meaning, side by side.

A Witch's Dream Tools: Enhancing Your Dream Work

There are several tools available to the dedicated dream worker, and Witches may already be familiar with many of them. There is tarot, of course, a virtual treasure box of rich imagery and symbolism, Association, Active Imagination, and Automatic Writing. Each one of these tools is a way to access the subconscious and trigger your intuitive abilities to uncover the hidden meanings of your dream language. Let us first look at tarot.

Tarot

As you grow in your understanding of archetypal symbols and the hidden energies that drive personality, begin to work with your tarot deck in dream work. If a strong image or personality emerges in your dream, seek out the corresponding figure within your tarot deck. For instance, if you have dreamt of the Fool, take that card and sit with it. Read various interpretations about the Fool's role in spiritual progress. Acquaint yourself with his function in our collective society, then meditate on how the Fool may be guiding you. What aspect of him is manifesting in you, in your life? Are you feeling a little foolish, or lost, not sure of where to begin? This is the Fool's energy—innocent, ready, but bumbling. Take heart, the Fool is all of us, the archetypal Pilgrim. His innocence is not a detriment, but a gift. How often have you heard that in order to reach enlightenment you must become like a child—naive, expectant, open to wonder, open to *possibility?*

In dreams we may meet many archetypal energies, from the gray-haired king to the beautiful maiden. Find the corresponding images in your tarot and work with them. Tarot and its powerful symbols emerged from the collective long ago, expressing truths about human nature in images and archetypes. Volumes have been written about the wisdom of tarot. There is not space enough in this book to cover all of its riches. Let me simply encourage you to open to the possibility of including the tarot deck in your dream work by intuitively seeking the cards that feel "charged" with your dream image. Meditate and open yourself to the meaning.

Association

To understand the language of dreams is to grasp the nonlinear, nonverbal "association" our subconscious infuses into our dream symbols. One possible way to access the meaning of a dream symbol is by using the process called Association.

Association is very simple. To begin, with a friend, go to a quiet, secluded spot. (Or try this in your own Dream Circle.) Give your friend a short list of your choice dream symbols (such as kitten, cave, sunglasses, or wallet). Sit quietly. Breathe! Have your friend start by saying aloud one of the words that identifies a dream symbol. Then, quickly respond without thinking about it. Say the first word that pops into your head. Your friend, in turn, will repeat that word back to you. You again respond with the next word, without analyzing. Simply say the first word that comes to you each time. And each time, have your friend repeat the last response back to you. Within a few words you will arrive at a word that surprises you. If you feel a chill, a sudden "Aha," you have found your association. It's quite intriguing. You may start with a word like *broom* and end up with *ancient fire*, as I did! You never know!

If you are alone and wish to try this, find a quiet spot and sit with your pen and paper. Take a deep breath. Hold the pen in your nondominant hand (the hand you usually do *not* write with) and, aloud, ask yourself to associate. Say aloud the first word symbol from your dream, and write down the first word that pops into your head. It should flow from your hand. Continue the association until you feel a "charge" on one of your written responses. Using your nondominant hand helps you to connect more directly to your subconscious. Let your intuition guide you.

Active Imagination

As we begin to recognize the myriad distinct energies that exist within our subconscious, we may then initiate a dialogue with these various dynamics, engaging them in an exchange and flow of information. Active Imagination, developed by Carl Jung, is a process similar to Association and shamanic journeying. It takes the waking dreamer into an imaginative alpha state, receptive and interactive. As the dreamer allows an image to rise from the subconscious, the dreamer can begin a dialogue with the image, asking questions, expressing feelings, and allowing the image to respond in its own wisdom. Often the thoughts and concepts expressed are startling to the dreamer, as the unknown parts of the self arise and make themselves "known." This is, in actuality, the purpose of dreams—to reveal the unknown to the known self. By practicing Active Imagination, Witches can enhance the dreaming process and deepen their inner awareness.

If you are alone, find a comfortable, safe place to sit quietly. Using a pen and paper to record your dialogue, begin with the pen in your nondominant hand. Start by visualizing a dream image or a word that holds meaning for you. Close your eyes and breathe deeply. Allow the image to rise and float before you. If the image speaks to you, begin to write down the message. Ask questions and write down the responses. Remember, this is a dialogue, and you are exploring an unknown part of your own self through this communication.

Sometimes the image will ask you to participate in some way, joining in with action. For example, I once had an Active Imagination experience during intense body work where my little girl (my inner child self) handed me a beautiful pair of Celtic engraved silver scissors. "What are these for?" I asked her. "To cut the cords embedded in your shoulder blades," she said, matter-of-factly. She then "showed me" two thick ropey cords hooked into my back. "They're connected to (this person)," she explained. "You had to carry too much responsibility." With tears in my eyes, I visualized myself turning around and readily snipping the cords. Active Imagination can be revealing, startling, and healing.

If you would prefer to have a guide with you on your inner journey, ask a friend to be with you. They will hold the pen and paper and record your session. Again, sit quietly, breathe, and begin allowing the image to rise within your mind's eye. Your partner may help guide you with gentle questions such as "Who is there with you?" "What do they look like?" "What are they saying?" "How do you feel?" By having a partner guide you, you are free to sit back, close your eyes, and allow your partner to record the journey. Let the images flow and take you on an exploration of your dreamscape. Allow the dialogue to unfold at its own pace.

If the images become frightening, remember that in facing our projected fears we dismantle the hold our fears have on us. The frightful image is only a projection of your own fear. Its gift is power, if you can summon the courage to face the fear and release it.

Automatic Writing

Another tool for dialoguing with your dream images is called Automatic Writing. By writing with our nondominant hand, we are able to access the subconscious. Sit quietly at a table or desk and light a white candle. Cast a simple circle of protection if you like, setting your psychic boundaries and clearly stating your intention of dialoguing with your own dream images. You are not inviting anybody else in to play!

Have pen and paper ready. Take a deep breath and close your eyes for a moment, bringing up your dream image. Ask your chosen dream image a question. Holding your pen in your nondominant hand, put your pen to the paper. Let the writing begin. If it doesn't start up right away, sometimes it helps to "loosen up" by squiggling some circles or doodles first, just to get the energy flowing from your hand into the pen. Once you start, don't stop. Keep writing. Do not worry about grammar or spelling.

I once had a remarkable Automatic Writing experience with a dream image who turned out to be my spiritual guide, my Daimon Lover. In dreams he had spoken no words at all, but simply stood there, with his unwavering gaze. Through writing, he spoke to me, revealing a wit and sense of irony that I had not expected at all. He even teased me!

Try one or all of these tools in conjunction with dream work. Explore which method works best for you. If you start your own Dream Circle, try experimenting with Association and Active Imagination. It's fun and always surprising.

8

Using Dream Symbols to Heal

As the previous dreams so clearly illustrate, our subconscious has the astonishing ability to reveal the underlying truth of ourselves, our relationships, struggles, and fears. We need only to pay close attention, to honor the revelations offered by writing them down, bringing our issues into the light of consciousness. In the simple act of acknowledging and journaling our dreams we begin healing ourselves and progressing toward wholeness. By working with *intention*, we are able to take this healing even further.

Witches work with the cyclic energies of the moon, sun, and seasons. Make note in your dream journal of the moon's phases. You may begin to notice your own patterns of dreaming and how they appear to correspond to the waxing and waning energy of the moon. Many dreamers report an increase in vivid dreaming as the moon waxes to fullness.

Working with the Moon

Distinct issues arise in dreams during the changing phases of the moon, even of the seasons. Dreamers have reported that during the darkening days of fall, they feel a psychic turn inward, and dreams become darker, deeper, more mysterious. Winter may bring a time of grounding, contemplation, and healing in the solitude offered by the cold ice moon. Spring may bring sexy dreams of love and desire, fueled by a growing sense of expansiveness and rebirth. Summer finds many dreamers drifting without any real inner work to do, their heated slumber prompting lighter, softer dreams reflecting daily life and outer relationships. A friend of mine reports that she does summer gardening in her sleep!

Work intentions with your dream symbols in concert with the moon's energies.

THE WANING MOON

During the waning moon, choose a dream symbol that reveals a need to let go of something. The decreasing moon is the perfect time for banishing an old habit or energy-draining addiction. If you need to let go of the "ties that bind" in an old relationship, the waning moon is the ideal moon phase to cut those lingering cords and break free; to bury the past hurts once and for all.

For a simple example: I might choose to work with the dream of my younger self in her frizzy home perm and patent leather shoes (discussed in chapter 2). I might look for a glossy magazine ad that promotes a similar view of femininity, something frilly pink and artificial. I could cut out the picture and place it in my cauldron. On an eve before the new moon, I would light a black candle for protection and truth, and set my intention to let go of the old bonds of childhood, the restraining pressures to conform to other's narrow concept of feminine beauty. I would burn cedar for cleansing and spiritual healing. Then I would burn the picture in my fireproof cauldron, watching the collective symbol of artificial beauty go up in smoke. I would then bury the ashes out in the garden, laying the outgrown to rest. Perhaps I would then treat myself to some sensuous music and a dance around the hearth, sipping a little sherry in celebration!

There are many ways to approach rituals of intention. They may be as simple as writing down that which you wish to banish on a small piece of paper and burning it, thus releasing the negative symbol. I could have found a pink barrette and simply buried it. Or taken a warm bath with sea salts (salt purifies and absorbs negativity) surrounded by candles (black for banishing) anointed with drops of rosemary and thyme oil. In a banishing bath, spend time visualizing the discarded expectations or unwanted aspects washing away, and let them swirl out of you and down into the drain as you unplug the tub! *Note:* If you choose to add essential oils to your bath, use caution, especially if you are pregnant or have skin sensitivities. Always consult a professional aromatherapist before using any oils other than lavender or tea tree oil.

Work with your dream symbols as simply or elaborately as you wish. Write a poem about it. Draw the dream out on a piece of paper. Burning or burying symbols of the negative and outgrown during the waning moon energy is extremely therapeutic, as well as magickal. Magick not only happens, it heals!

THE WAXING MOON

During the waxing moon we are blessed with an expanding, realizing energy, helping us move toward our full potential, fueling our growth and creative expression. Find a positive dream image that captures your desire toward healing, hope, a wish, a new venture or project, a new love . . . any possibility. Work with it. Make it a part of your everyday life. Write a short poem visualizing its potential and stick it on your bedroom mirror. Find a picture that represents a wish or desire and tack it up in your work space. Choose a figure in tarot to represent that which you wish to attract and place the card on your altar. (I met my soul mate that way!)

I like to write down my intentions, goals, and desires for each full moon and keep them tucked inside my wallet, which is always close at hand and accompanies me wherever I go.

Wallets carry coins, money, credit, and identification. Symbolically, a wallet contains things that we value, "proof" of who we are, so why should we not also carry our wishes, hopes, and dreams?

Celebrate possibility becoming reality. Inscribe a candle in the appropriate color and burn it on your altar. Find a visual image that expresses your dream and display it on your altar, surrounding it with flowers, herbs, and crystals. Burn cinnamon and mint for abundance, lavender for happiness, and sage for wisdom and protection.

Leave a small glass of wine or juice outside in the garden to give thanks to the Lord and Lady for helping to manifest your dream. And leave a tiny dish of treats for the fairies! (They like milk and cookies!) Feed the birds with seed. Leave a gift at your favorite tree.

Believe in your soul and its innate life force. Fill your heart with love and generosity, and open your life to all possibility. Accept healing and wholeness, and hold within the light of truth to guide your way. The Goddess is alive, and magick is afoot!

Our Separate Reality

In our superficial culture, we have been taught to believe that our waking life is our "real life," and our dreams are merely sleeping fantasies. The more I wrestle with dreams and work with other dreamers, the more I have realized that our *dreams* are truly our "real life." Our dreams are the journey of the soul.

Our waking life is far too often caught up in the illusion of the material world, its values and pressures, its addictions and distractions. Our dreams reveal to us the truth of our whole selves, our spirit, our progress, our past, our fears, our relationships. Dreams introduce us to our inner guides and give us a glimpse into possibility and eternity. Our dreams have the power to heal.

As Witches, we believe in this separate reality and honor the energies that dreams and visions hold. We feel a part of the whole of Nature, her web of interconnection, her electric pulse of opposites, her simple truths and profound lessons. In dreams we are able to catch a glimpse of what is possible, what is true, and what is magick. Let us honor such a gift!

9

STARTING YOUR OWN
DREAM CIRCLE

There *is*, indeed, something special about gathering a circle of women together for a purpose. (It may certainly be possible to form a mixed circle with men and women; however, I have only had experience with exclusively female Dream Circles.) In days past, women would routinely gather together to share in daily tasks such as laundry, marketing, and preparing foods. There they would discuss the day's difficulties, joys, and celebrations, from milestones to mere gossip. While I do not lament the easing of our manual household labors, I do believe that we postmodern women have lost something in the acquiring of our private modern conveniences: the community of women. The daily sense of sharing and support.

Whether we come together for quilting, a book discussion, a Sabbat, or the sharing of dreams, we create a sacred space that is separate from our daily routine. Through our stories and our insights we bond in empathy, weaving threads of connection and support. The revelations we share equal the laughter.

Starting a Dream Circle is an exciting adventure. Coming together for the intention of studying dreams and symbology awakens our access to the subconscious. In exploring dreams together we enhance the process of remembering, analyzing, and understanding the language of dreams. As we grow and learn together, we deepen our understanding of symbology and awaken to the complex beauty of our shared collective experience. The exchange of ideas and emotions raises our level of awareness and enhances our individual pathfinding.

To begin a Dream Circle, start with a close friend, discuss the idea, then approach a few other women friends you intuit might be receptive. As few as three women can be enough to start a circle. Four is my favorite number. I find that an evening flies by quickly with four dreamers sharing their dreams. Before you know it, three hours have passed! If you have six women who are avidly interested, this can also work well. Any more than that may lead to frustration, with not nearly enough time to share everyone's dreams.

How often you meet will be up to you. I host my Dream Circle twice a month, during the weeks of the new moon and the full moon. I have found that our rhythms of dreaming and insight respond to the changes of the moon, and we often will close our gathering in a brief ritual of banishing (during the waning moon) or intention (during the full moon week), whichever is appropriate. Many personal issues arise in dream work, and including the healing of ritual enhances our spiritual progress and understanding.

Trust is of utmost importance. Inviting women who are "trustworthy" sets a strong foundation for the growth of the group. Occasionally, personalities may irritate or feelings might get bruised, but if you establish a bond of trust right at the beginning, with true commitment from each woman, you should encounter little difficulty.

The format you create with your Dream Circle should reflect the group; some groups enjoy an easygoing free flow of an evening, with little structure. As long as each participant has an equal chance to share a dream with the group, this can work. One dreamer should be willing to guide the group, though, keeping things moving through the circle, so each person has their chance to share.

If you prefer a more structured approach, use this book as a guide and begin with a chapter each month, discussing archetypes the first month, Animus the next, shadow the next, and so on. Plan on lively discussion and hashing out opinions! Chapter 6, Beginning Your Dream Work, contains a guide that will help you through a discussion of each participant's dream. Ask the questions listed to prompt an exploration of ideas. As people become familiar with dream symbology, it can be an exciting journey to decipher a dream together.

If you feel confident as the leader, you can also initiate some of the Witch's Tools and try, for example, Association or Automatic Writing with the group. Use your imagination and intuition to guide you. If a ritual seems appropriate, include a banishing or an intention ritual at the close of a Dream Circle, touching upon issues that were brought up during the evening. Something as simple as writing down a desire on paper, whether to banish or intend, and then burning it in a cauldron together can be an inspirational end to an evening.

In our Dream Circle we have shared banishing, healing, and cleansing rituals. Once, at the turn of the New Year, we all took turns washing our hands, and faces, too, in a beautiful large bowl. Lavender and thyme candles softly glowed, and ivory linen hand towels were passed out to dry fingers and tears. Rituals help to bind the trust of the circle, as well as to enhance the work being done.

As with any circle gathering, be sure to include some food and drink! In our circle, the women "pay" me for hosting with boxes of herb teas and baked edibles for the group. I usually supply a large bowl of fresh hot popcorn and a steaming tea kettle, and, on occasion, sweet treats, from homemade fudge brownies to lavender cookies. We've also been known to sip a little sherry now and then (mind you, we're all the *legal age* for such a pleasure).

A Dream Circle is a rewarding, enhancing, and inspiring experience. It has been an enormous gift in my life. I have been privileged to host a circle of women whose devotion to the truth, willingness to share, take risks, and support one another has truly inspired the writing of this book. I am grateful to each one of them. We have shared both laughter and tears. May this book encourage you to reach out and do the same; to begin your own Dream Circle and journey together into the magickal and inspiring beauty of dreams.

10

A Witch's Dream Dictionary

To help you get started on your journey into dream work, I have included my own dream dictionary, which provides symbols and concepts culled from personal and shared dreams, as well as from research I have collected for over two decades. My intent in offering you these interpretations is to familiarize you with the universal language of dreams, collective concepts, and common symbols. As always, I encourage you to apply your own personalized viewpoint to the interpretations, shading the meaning with your own emotional response.

Enter this dictionary with an open mind and an open heart, allowing your intuition to guide you. No single definition is absolute. No solitary viewpoint is written in stone. Dream work is soul work and, as such, asks of each one of us to begin with clear intention and an open spirit.

Take time to browse through the entire dictionary and familiarize yourself with an overview of symbols. If you are looking up one particular meaning, check the associated words and symbols I often include at the end of each entry. Follow the thread of images and words that have woven your dream, as they will often lead you to a place you would never expect. As we Witches realize, the journey *is the destination*.

ABYSS

Standing at the edge of an abyss may symbolize facing a life-changing decision, making a leap of faith into the unknown. The future may feel uncertain. The depth of the crevasse reflects your fear. Or, do you feel exhilaration? *See* Bridge.

ACCIDENT

Seeing an accident in a dream may be a warning; are you headed for catastrophe? Is a situation in your life an "accident waiting to happen"? Our subconscious mind is often able to see into future outcomes more readily than our ego mind. Or perhaps you feel that you've been emotionally scarred by a "hit and run" relationship?

AIR

One of the four elements, air is linked to mental activity, the realm of the mind; concept, thought, abstraction. Are you exploring new ideas? Rising to a mental challenge? Read up on the suit of Swords in tarot, representing the air element. *See* Wind.

AIRPLANE

Dreaming of being on an airplane is symbolic of traveling to new horizons, covering new territory. Perhaps you have embarked on a new project, or have moved forward in your pursuit of a goal. You are now on your way. Flying high. *See* Airport; Baggage.

AIRPORT

A place of transition, changes coming; you are about to go (progress) somewhere else, move in a different direction, and are preparing to *take off*. *See* Airplane; Baggage.

ALARM

A possible warning, do you hear it? Are you listening? Your subconscious may be trying to wake you, shake you up, signaling you to take notice—now!

ALCHEMY

Alchemy was a mystical process by which an ordinary base metal was placed inside a vessel and mysteriously converted into precious gold. This is a perfect symbol for our own inner transformation: The vessel symbolizes the container of the self, the base metal is our fledgling unconscious psyche. Through an enigmatic magical process, our "raw material" becomes gold, our true synthesized whole self, shining, light (conscious).

ALCOHOL

Also known as spirits, alcohol can symbolize exactly that. Drinking in spirits is a longing to be filled with the spiritual. Addiction to alcohol is a powerful need to be filled spiritually, with the addict feeling as if they can never be filled (fulfilled). See Wine.

ALIEN

Representing a being totally foreign, unknown, and unfamiliar, an alien may portray an unknown, unacknowledged aspect of yourself. A part of yourself you may be afraid to embrace. See Shadow; Spaceship.

ALTAR

A focal point for reverence and worship, a sacred place, a center for ritual and magick, an altar may represent the sacred space within you. A place of ceremony and sacrament. Also, possibly your physical body, depending upon the dream.

AMULET

A charm created with intention, infused with the energy and focus of the creator. Amulets for protection, fertility, or attraction, for example, can be held, carried, and worn. Are you holding an amulet? Being given one? Have you lost your amulet? Think about the symbology of what the charm represented. If it was protection, for instance, perhaps you are having anxiety about feeling safe, or your subconscious mind is urging you to create some protection energy around you. If you've lost the amulet in your dream, you are feeling exposed and vulnerable, "without protection."

ANCHOR

Dreaming of an anchor indicates you are feeling secure, rooted, connected. If you dream of looking for a spot to throw your anchor, you are searching for such a connection, a safe harbor. *See* Boat; Lake; Ocean.

ANIMA

A man's inner feminine soul twin that reveals herself in his dreams. She may appear as a maiden, a muse, a lover, a partner. She exemplifies his inner feminine, his intuition, creativity, connection to nature, to others, to the life force. She is his inspiration. Through maturity, growth, and balance, a man will embrace his inner feminine aspect and become whole. How she appears in his dreams will be a clue as to his regard for her. *See* Lover; Model; Muse.

ANIMALS

Often representing the more instinctual, natural aspects of oneself, an animal may describe one's pure emotions, appetite, urges, or intuitive nonverbal nature. Animals can also be spiritual allies, guiding us in our dream state. At times, depending upon the animal's traits, it may signify a compulsion. Look up specific animals for more individual associations.

ANIMUS

A woman's inner masculine soul twin that reveals himself in dreams. He may appear as a strong youth, a guide, a teacher, a lover. He delineates her inherent spiritual muscle; the courage to speak up, share ideas, initiate projects, work in the world, venturing into the realm of ideas and self-expression. As the Daimon Lover, he may show up as a mysterious guide holding a lantern in the dark passage for the dreamer to see her soul path more clearly. Through maturity, growth, and balance, a woman will embrace her masculine aspect and become whole. How he appears in her dreams will be a clue as to how developed he is within her. *See* Daimon; Lover.

ANKH

An ancient Egyptian symbol symbolizing immortality, and the key to unlocking the great mysteries. How the ankh appeared in your dream will give you a clue to its meaning. Were you holding it, about to use it to enter a doorway? You have found the key to unlocking an unknown aspect of yourself.

ANTIQUE SHOP/ANTIQUES

A shop indicates opportunity and choices. Being in an antique shop is exploring the past; seeking out the valuable, the splendid, the old ways, arcane knowledge, precious or sacred objects, elements of the past that are worth retrieving. *See* Shopping.

ANTLERS

The trophy, the prize for the hunt, representing masculine energy; associated with the Stag, Herne, the King of the Forest. Power and virility. At Beltane the male celebrants wear antlers to symbolize this masculine procreative power. *See* Horned One; Stag.

APARTMENTS

A structure, a dwelling that houses many different people. Perhaps this is about finding your separate self, differentiating yourself from the collective mind. A structure or shelter completely separate of your own would perhaps indicate your autonomy and set boundaries. *See* Building; House; Office.

APPLE

One of the favored fruits of the Goddess, symbolizing knowledge or wisdom. The apple (crosscut) contains the five-pointed star that is sacred to the Goddess, the pentagram. In a Christian context, an apple can symbolize temptation, the forbidden, Eve's urge toward knowledge and discernment. *See* Fruit; Goddess.

ARCHETYPE

Emerging from our shared Collective Unconscious, archetypes are manifestations of human traits and truths, representing our impulses and behavior patterns, our experiences, conflicts, weaknesses, and strengths. Archetypes can be found in myth, fairy tales, stories, movies, comics, religion, tarot, even television. Dreaming of a particular celebrity may be dreaming of an archetypal energy that this celebrity embodies, as our culture pushes such visual archetypal symbols into our line of vision every day. Romantic Heroes such as Keanu Reeves and Johnny Depp stare back at us from magazines and billboards. Reluctant Hero Harrison Ford, Bad Boy Brad Pitt, and Jim Carrey as the Fool/Clown vie with actresses such as Cameron Diaz and Julia Roberts, who embody the Maiden archetype. Ads, television, and the Internet bombard us daily with such images and archetypal types. Concepts such as birth, death, justice, and revenge are also archetypal, triggering an inner emotional response. See chapter 1, Understanding Archetypes, for a more in-depth look at how archetypal energies work.

ARMOR

A suit of armor or plate of armor is protection, feeling the need to shield oneself, making oneself invincible. Preparing for battle. Are you facing a conflict? *See* Battle; Grail; King; Knight; Sword.

ARROW

An arrow signifies the ability to penetrate to the heart of the matter, to focus, to hit your target or goal. *See* Battle; Bow and Arrow; Hunt.

ARMY

See Collective.

ATHAME

A sacred tool for ritual, used to delineate a circular space, separating the sacred from the mundane world. Do you need to create some sacred space in your life? Or make some difficult decisions regarding how you place your energy? Use the athame symbolically to mentally cut away that which is no longer suitable and create a sense of the sacred in your life. Claim your space. Use the power of your mind, thoughts, the element of air, and the athame to help you become clear. Set your boundaries. *See* Air; Dagger; Knife; Sword.

AURA

The light that emits around living beings; an energy field. You may be increasing your awareness of these energies or discovering how to see them. Perhaps it is simply confirmation of the fact that we are all made up of bundles of energy; we are all beings of light. In your dream state you are more receptive to see this truth.

BABY

Giving birth to an infant can symbolize a new beginning, the birth of a new aspect of oneself, a brand new idea, or a creative project. A Divine Child or Wonder Baby, one who walks and talks, is an archetypal image signifying the birth of the divine within us, the new son/sun of hope emerging. Very positive. *See* Archetypes.

BACK

Play with word phrases: going back, get back, back out, back up, getting back into, "I'm back," "Back me up," watch your back. Or is it about a backbone, a spine, a willingness to stand up for what you believe in?

BAGGAGE

Are you loaded down with excess baggage? What are you clinging to or dragging along with you? Parts of the past? Old hurts? Old "dirty laundry"? Clothes that don't fit anymore? (Aspects of identity that you've outgrown?) What is burdening you or weighing you down? *See* Airplane; Airport; Car; Driving; Train.

BALCONY

Standing on a balcony, looking upon a vista may mean that you need to have a higher perspective, to see more of what lies "out there" in the distance. Get a grasp of the bigger picture. Or perhaps you are feeling a bit *above it all* these days? *See* Up.

BANDAGE/BAND-AID

Is there a wound that needs time to heal? An injury? Are you nursing a hurt? A Band-Aid covers the wound, are you covering up a hurt? Is your wound a badge of courage? Do you identify yourself as *wounded*? *See* Accident; Blood; Hospital; Violence; Wound.

BARRIER

Encountering an obstacle to your progress; something is in your way. How do you need to approach this barrier? If you are climbing up, it may be about an obstacle to your spiritual progress, to seeking consciousness. If the barrier is keeping you from descending, going down into the depths, into the dark, you may be encountering a problem with facing the unknown, keeping yourself from exploring the unfamiliar, deeper aspects of yourself. This barrier would be denial.

BASEMENT

The lower level basement suggests the subconscious, the underlying mindfulness that hides underneath. The inner, darker place within our psyche. The house is a symbol of the self; therefore, the basement, or cellar, is an appropriate symbol for the lesser-known elements of ourselves. Things are hidden and put away down in the basement. It is the perfect symbolic place to store old family issues, fears, bad memories, and those things we try to avoid. Stairs going down into the basement signify access to the subconscious. When dreamers first begin exploring dream work, there are often dreams of walking down stairs to the dark cellar, going down to find and retrieve something in their subconscious. *See* Dark; Down; Home/House; Ladder; Stairs.

BASKET

Connected to the feminine by virtue of its ability to contain, a basket is symbolic of woman, the Goddess energy, and the gifts that femininity brings. Is the basket full of goodies (gifts), or is it empty, waiting to be filled? This could indicate a reflection on whether you feel fulfilled, or void, waiting to be completed.

BATH

Cleansing; washing away. Purification. Water is the emotions; tears are shed to cleanse the heart. A bath can be a ritual, a place of peace and quiet. An inner journey to the self. The figure Star in tarot is often in a cleansing pool. Are you exploring your emotional depths? *See* Washing; Water.

BATHROOM

Going to the bathroom dreams are very common as dreamers begin to assimilate dream work and work on issues of the self, learning and sorting through, then eliminating a lot of what they no longer need. Getting rid of waste. Letting it go, flushing it away. Proof that our subconscious has a sense of humor! *See* Vomiting.

BATTLE

You are in battle with an inner aspect of yourself. Are you in conflict? What parts of you are fighting for the upper hand? Who are you fighting with? Your shadow, a parent, a sibling? Their identity clues you in to the aspect of yourself or your values that are in conflict. *See* Knight; Violence; War.

BAZAAR

See Marketplace.

BEAM

A ray of light, a shining beam is power and energy. Where is this beam of light coming from? It may be healing, or infusing you with power. *See* Light.

BEAR

A multifaceted symbol, a bear is about earth medicine, knowledge of herbs and roots, a maternal instinct and fierce protection. Also, in hibernation, the bear's message is to go within and find stillness and solitude. We sometimes need a time of hibernation to nurture our weary spirit.

BEAVER

An industrious animal, busy and goal oriented. Do you need to get going on a project and stop putting it off? Or are you overworking, getting caught up in the details? Are you damming up the flow of feelings? Or energy? Are you compulsive in your work habits?

BED

Your place of rest, safety, relationship (lovemaking), a bed may be about your level of intimacy, your sense of security, your marriage or relationship to a partner. Are you asleep in the dream, unconscious? Are you hiding out under the bedcovers? Is there a stranger in your bed? (An unknown aspect of yourself threatening your sense of security?) It may be time to wake up and smell the coffee. *See* Room.

BEES

Industrious, communal, hardworking, and selfless, bees can signify work, joining in a cause, contributing to the common good. Have you been "busy as a bee" lately? Bees' natural protection is their ability to sting. Have you been stung by someone or some situation? Or has a stinging remark hurt your pride?

BEETLE

An ancient symbol from the East Mediterranean, the beetle, or scarab, signifies renewal and regeneration. Is the beetle in your dream there to remind you of the cycles of life, death, and rebirth?

BESOM

A Witch's sacred tool, the besom is symbolic of connection to the Goddess, the feminine ways, the Old Folk Ways. Used to *sweep and clear* negative energy, to create a clean space for magickal workings, the besom is a beloved tool. Perhaps you are needing to make a clean sweep of things, or create a sacred space for yourself. *See* Broom/Broomstick; Witch.

BICYCLE

Riding a bike is you moving forward under your own power, going in the direction you choose in life. Or it can be escape, flying like the wind, away. A throwback to the early freedoms of youth. How do you feel on your bike? Where are you headed? Is it an uphill struggle, or smooth sailing? If the road is clogged with traffic, perhaps you feel the interference of the collective. If you are cycling apart from the crowd, you are pursuing your own path. *See* Path; Road.

BIRDS

Spiritual, sky bound, birds are symbols of freedom and the air element, riding on the wind, above the earthbound, seeing things from a higher perspective. Birds can be messengers and bring warnings. Celtic Goddesses and Native American Medicine People had the ability to shapeshift into birds, especially crows, and escape danger. Check listings for individual birds for specific traits. *See* Animals.

BIRTH
See Baby.

BISON
See Buffalo.

BITE
The bite of a snake is initiation. The power to die and be reborn. The piercing initiates the dreamer into the spiritual shamanic realm. The gateway to the journey. Or are you doing the biting? Biting off more than you can chew? Biting the hand that feeds you? *See* Bullet; Vampire.

BLACK
The direction *west* associates black with death and sorrow. Eastern belief systems see black as representing time; in Egypt it is the color of rebirth. Witches believe that wearing black is protective, as black absorbs negative energy and deflects it. Note your feelings around the presence of black in your dream. To some black can signify a dark mood or depression.

BLACK MADONNA
See Madonna.

BLOOD
The rich red stuff of life itself. Losing blood can symbolize losing your vital life energy, feeling drained. Blood is a mystery, a sacred bond, the color of wine. Menstrual blood is full of power, a symbol

for the strength and archetypal energy of the divine feminine. *See* Goddess; Vampire; Wound.

BLUE

The color blue is associated with the sky, spirituality, and peace; the deep blue sea. It stands for calm and quiet strength. It invites dreams and daydreams, clarity and ease. Blue corresponds to the throat chakra, the energy gateway of speech and self-expression. Speaking one's truth.

BOAT

A boat can be a symbol of the self, a soul vessel on top of the great depths of the subconscious. Is it rocky and turbulent? Are you having trouble navigating the rough waters of your life right now? If the sea is calm, the boat signifies safe passage, the means to cross to the other side, where there will be peace. *See* Anchor; Lake; Ocean; Sailing.

BOOKS

Books are symbols of knowledge and wisdom. And knowledge is power. Contemporary Witches often educate themselves through voracious reading. A collection of books can mean a wealth of knowledge, ancient secrets, a desire for learning, growth, and development. A Book of Shadows signifies hidden knowledge and the key to the mysteries. *See* Library.

BONDS

If there are shackles around your wrists or ankles, some belief is binding you, holding you back, curtailing your freedom of expression and movement. If it is a financial (paper) bond representing stocks, it is about an investment you have made. Are you receiving dividends on your investment? (We can invest our time, energy, faith, love, and attention.) Has it paid off? Perhaps you are questioning that.

BONES

Finding bones can mean uncovering ancient heritage and power. Unearthing our ancestors, our origins. It can also mean something is stripped to the bare bones, to its essentials. What have you discovered? See Buried; Death; Grave; Skull.

BOW AND ARROW

A bow and arrow is the power to be on the mark, to focus your energies and aim at a target, or goal. Are you hitting your objective? Have you missed? Try again. See Arrow; Hunt/Hunting.

BREAD

The staff of life, a gift from the Mother Goddess of grain, and the God of the fields, John Barleycorn. Breaking bread, sharing food with someone is symbolic of friendship and cooperation. It creates a bond between those who partake. Perhaps you are bonding with a new aspect of yourself. If you are sharing food (nurturing knowledge/information), you are in cooperation with different parts/roles of your life. See Food.

BREASTS

A symbol of the nurturing maternal feminine, the Great Goddess, provider. Breasts can also be erotic, an aspect of feminine beauty. Sucking on breasts may be a desire to be nurtured on an emotional level. Connected with the Goddess it can mean being fed spiritually by the divine feminine. See Food; Goddess; Milk; Mother.

BRIDGE

A crossing over, a transition to a new place, a connection to the future, or to the next phase of life. Passing from one realm into the next. Taking the risk to make the crossing can take courage and diligence. If there are gaps or holes in the bridge, you may feel as if you are not fully supported in this change, and fear may be holding you back. See Abyss; Falling; Path; River.

BROOM/BROOMSTICK

An implement to sweep the space clear, to get rid of the cobwebs, the dust, and negativity. Perhaps your psychic space needs to be cleaned out. Do you need to psychically clean house? Or do you just feel like going for a ride? *See* Besom; Witch.

BROTHER

Dreaming of one's brother, if you are a female, may symbolize the masculine side of your self. If you are a male and dream of your brother, it may indicate that you are meeting your shadow, the aspect of yourself that carries qualities and traits that you deny and keep hidden from the outside world. *See* Animus; Child; Shadow; Youth.

BUFFALO

The buffalo meant sustenance for the western Plains People and has come to symbolize abundance because of the many gifts the buffalo brings. This spiritual symbol in a dream is a powerful one, signifying the prosperity, bounty, and hope that this noble animal once offered to North America's indigenous people.

BUILDING

Working on creating something, building a new life, or crafting a new idea or concept of the self. Creating a new dimension of yourself, new psychic space. The noun *building* (structure), is related to the self. *See* Apartments; Door; Entry; Hallway; Home/House; Hotel; Renovate; Room; Stairs; Wall; Window.

BULL

Massive imposing physical strength characterizes the bull, as do the associations of stubbornness and determination. Look at what the bull was doing in your dream. Were you cooperating with it, or frightened by it? Perhaps it represents a part of your personality or strong natural impulse. It may represent an insensitive and over-bearing aspect of yourself (or someone in your life).

BULLET

A surprise, sudden change, fierce speed, a threat. Perhaps you are feeling under the gun, under pressure. The time to act is now. Or are you biting the bullet, putting up with something you find distasteful, enduring?

BURGLAR

Dreaming of a dark threatening intruder is symbolic of fearing to face one's shadow, the archetypal Stranger, the unknown self. If left unacknowledged, the shadow becomes an unwanted visitor, intruding into your house/self, threatening to enter uninvited. Ignoring your shadow aspect will *steal* your energy. Facing our dark side is a big step toward integration of the self. *See* Dark; Home/House; Shadow.

BURIED

If something is buried, it has been intentionally hidden away, put out of sight. "Out of sight, out of mind," the saying goes. To dig for buried treasure is to search for an aspect of yourself long ago stuffed away. To bury something in your dream is about getting rid of an aspect and putting it to rest. To bury the hatchet is to make peace with one's enemy. Sometimes we are our own worst. *See* Earth; Grave; Under; Yard.

BUTTERFLY

Transformation and metamorphosis. The completion of the journey. Beauty in flight, happiness, and lightness. Lack of concerns. Have you recently emerged from a dark phase of cocooning and isolation? Moths are also a symbol of the soul in many cultures.

BUYING

Acquiring something new, taking an opportunity in hand. Is the price high? Are you able to pay the price for this new possibility? You must decide whether you are acquiring something of value, or merely an article with little substance. Buying clothing may indicate examining a new aspect of your identity and how you present yourself to others. *See* Coins; Marketplace; Money; Shopping; Wallet.

CABIN

A safe haven, retreat, or structure of the self. Where is it? And how is it furnished? Note if it is bare and empty, or brimming full. Dirty and disorganized, or comfortable and welcoming. Your cabin reflects who you are, and what your current mental state is. *See* Building; Home/House; Forest; Weather.

CAGE

Conceivably you are feeling trapped, restricted, without freedom. What is this cage in your life or your inner self? Look for clues as to what it is that is holding you back, keeping you separated from truly experiencing life. *See* Lock; Key.

CAKE

A treat, desert, celebration, or something forbidden and nonnutritional. Examine your feelings about food. What associations do you attribute to eating cake? Perhaps this dream is about enjoying your cake (pleasure). Do you deny yourself? Maybe you simply need more sweetness in your disposition. A birthday cake could signify a milestone, a rite of passage in your growth. Note the flavor, and your associations to it. Do you love chocolate? Or is it a forbidden food? *See* Food.

CANDLE

A spiritual symbol for many, especially for the Witch. The candle represents the masculine element of fire, warmth, and light. Magick and spirit. A flame can mean faith, devotion, hope, even love, burning brightly within you. Light is illumination and inspiration. Are you tending your inner flame? *See* Dark; Fire; Lantern; Light.

CAR

Driving a car is indicative of how you are moving forward in your life; the road you are taking, how well you are negotiating and maneuvering. Is your car safe and comfortable, or cramped, run down, a rattletrap? (This helps to indicate how well you have prepared yourself for your journey.) If you are driving, you are feeling in control of your destiny. If someone else is at the wheel taking charge of your destination, you are experiencing a loss of control. Your car symbolizes your ability to get from here to there. *See* Landscape; Road; Weather.

CAT

Often a favorite familiar of the Witch, the feline is mystery and knowledge, an ally, one who shares secrets. Independent and beautiful. Feminine instinct, a hunter, a seeker of comfort. Inscrutable. Do you have a cat in your life? This dream cat may reflect an aspect of your own feline instinct. If the cat is wounded, a part of your instinctual feminine is wounded. Are you rescuing the cat (your natural instinct)? Feeding it? (Nurturing your intuition?) If the cat has given birth to kittens, renewed feminine instinct/intuition is being born within you.

CAULDRON

A vessel of transformation, the receptacle of the Goddess, the divine feminine. A cauldron is the container for all of your hopes, wishes, and dreams, your connection to the ancient ways of the Goddess. The place of alchemy and transformation. *See* Alchemy; Cooking; Fire; Goddess; Hearth; Witch.

CAVE

A place of safety, a refuge in Mother Earth. An ancient dwelling, a place of the Goddess. A place of shelter. The home of the bear and the leopard. Perhaps you need to hibernate and ground yourself. Or conceivably you are exploring your feminine subconscious, excavating your ancient roots. Is this a ceremony? Initiation into the mysteries of Gaia, Mother Earth? (Gaia, also spelled Gaea, was the Greek name for Mother Earth, the Great Goddess.) *See* Dark; Earth; Goddess; Mother.

CELLAR

See Basement.

CELTIC CROSS

The Celtic Cross predates Christianity by several centuries. In its original symbolism, the upright cross stood for the *masculine* aspect, the enclosing circle for the *feminine*, making it indicative of fertility and the balance of male/female. Perhaps you are achieving a balance in your own male and female characteristics, finding the presence of both the God and the Goddess in your spirituality.

CHAKRAS

Jungians refer to the system of seven chakras as "energy gateways to the body." Chakras correspond to seven centers in the body, from the root chakra at the base of the spine, upward to the crown chakra at the top of the head. Learning about these energy gateways helps us to use the body's energy flow and receive information and healing from magick and nature. Chakras correspond to specific emotional issues and can become blocked by unexplored or repressed response and trauma. Self-healing through chakra work and meditation helps Witches to clear their energy pathway and channel their power. See appendix A to learn more about correspondences.

CHALICE

A receptacle, the feminine principle, a sacred cup, the holy grail. What are you receiving? Are you being filled? Feeling empty? Are you spiritually thirsty? Are you sharing the chalice, your spiritual gift? See Altar; Cup; Grail; Wine.

CHILD/CHILDREN

Young children can often exemplify a younger aspect of oneself, perhaps a part of us that we have left behind in order to be grown up. Perhaps you are in the process of reclaiming your inner child, or some long-forgotten aptitude. If we are drawn to taking care of the child, we may be returning to a psychological stage when we were hurt in our young life, helping to heal an early wound to the psyche. If the child is playful, it might indicate that we need to take more time to play and enjoy life, getting back in touch with our more innocent joys. See Archetype; Youth.

CIRCLE

One of the first symbols, a primal and powerful archetype of the self. A circle is spiritual, embodying wholeness and completion. A mandala to enter in contemplation. It also represents the wheel of life, the wheel of the seasons, and the four directions. A circle is *cast* for protection in ritual, defining a sacred space. It can represent the primary shape of the sun and the full moon. Contemplate its simplicity and completion. See Archetype; Athame; Goddess; Witch.

CITY

Dense, busy, hectic, buzzing with people, movement, and diverse energies. A city may represent the confusion and density of the collective mind itself. The distraction of modern life, the noise and the visual stimulation. Do you thrive on it? Or do you feel the need to escape to more a quiet, natural environment? See Collective; Day; Landscape; Night; Weather.

CLIMBING

Climbing upward in dreams can be symbolic of your progress, your ascent toward spiritual and creative goals. Do you feel as if you are indeed making progress, or are you slipping, finding it difficult to secure your footing? Perhaps there are boulders (obstacles) in your way. Ask yourself what is getting in the way of your progress. *See* Bridge; Building; Ladder; Mountain; Path; Stairs; Up; Wall.

CLINGING

Hanging on for dear life, grasping for a sure hold, may indicate that you are clinging to something that no longer serves you. Holding on to the right things for valid reasons is one thing. But clinging to worn-out ideals and beliefs that no longer serve your spirit is impeding your growth. Is what you are clinging to crumbling in your hands? Perhaps you should let go. Are you afraid to let go? Afraid you will not be supported?

CLOTHES

Clothing represents our persona, our image that we project to the world, how we see ourselves and wish others to see us. What is your style? Are you happy with the identity you've chosen? Maybe you need a change. If you are taking clothes off and discarding, you are getting rid of old outworn identities, peeling away your layers. If you are washing the clothing, you are busy cleaning up your image. Fixing or mending clothes indicates your desire to improve your image and repair any flaws that you see in your self-presentation. *See* Costume; Hat; Mask; Sewing; Shoes; Washing.

CLOCK

Time . . . our awareness of it. Perhaps you are feeling as if you are running out of time, or running late. Is this your biological clock? Maybe you wish you had some time out for awhile.

CLOSET

The obvious association is that one hides things in a closet, storing them away from sight. A dark concealed place. A space to keep secrets. The phrase "out of the closet" has come to mean exposing the truth about oneself. Now, if it's a *broom closet*, my darlings, you *know* what this means!

CLOUDS

Clouds are a complex symbol. Being a part of the sky and air above, they have a connection to the spirit, to lofty ideals, to heaven, to an otherworldly realm. Or they may mean cloudy thinking. Are you clouded by doubt? Is your judgment clouded these days? Are you seeing things clearly? Filled with rain, they may signify sorrows. A rainstorm may embody the healing act of letting loose pent-up emotions. *See* Landscape; Sky; Water; Weather.

CLOWN

See Archetypes; Fool.

COINS

A means of exchange. The price you pay. What something is valued at. The material, the earth element, pentacles. Worth. *See* Gold; Money; Pentacles; Silver; Wallet.

COLLECTIVE

Briefly, dreaming of the collective is dreaming of the prevailing shared viewpoint of the culture you live in. Your dreams may reflect your conflict with this collective view. Often dreamers who are independent thinkers, finding their own path, may struggle with breaking away from their cultural collective and the pervasive pressure to conform. Media symbols such as models, television stars, athletes, and ads may all represent the collective ideal, as well as sports arenas, teams, groups, uniforms, and flags that identify one with a group perspective. If the dream makes you feel left out or under pressure to conform, in style or beliefs, or features a group mind, such as a team or army, you can suspect the dream is about your relationship to the collective. Most Witches find themselves feeling outside the mainstream, apart from the ideals of the collective Judeo-Christian group mind. Read chapter 1, Understanding Archetypes, to learn more about the concept of the collective. *See* Archetypes; Army; Court; Game; Group; Jury.

COLORS

Colors can have significant meanings. If you remember a very particular color in the dream, it may relate to the mystical meaning of that specific color, associated with energy centers in the body (the chakras) or the emotional correlation of colors. Look up the specific color in this dictionary, and read appendix A for more information.

COOKING

Cooking is transformation, using heat (energy) to change something into a form that is palatable, digestible. Perhaps it is about taking in information/knowledge in a way that is easier for you to digest. *See* Alchemy; Cauldron; Food; Kitchen; Stove.

CORD

That which connects and binds. Perhaps you need to cut the cord to a person or relationship. Is something binding you, holding you in, keeping you from pursuing your freedom? If the cord is an electrical one, this may symbolize your connection to power. *See* Knot; Tying.

CORN

Symbolizing fertility, corn was thought to be the offspring of the union of sun and earth. Food can also mean nutrition, nourishment. The care and feeding of ideas. What is feeding you in a spiritual sense?

COSTUME

Wearing a costume in a dream can be about trying on a new identity, seeing how it fits. It can also be a way to hide oneself, disguising the truth of who you are. Does it feel fake to wear it? Or liberating? The kind of costume it is, the era, the style will give you clues as to what identity you are playing around with. Just who do you want to be?

COURT

A playing court can be an arena of performance. Are you anxious about your performance out in the world? Are you feeling under pressure to score points, to win? Are the spectators cheering you on or booing? (Are you feeling supported or rejected?) A legal court can mean something else entirely. Are you standing before a judge, being judged? Perhaps you are being held accountable for something by your conscience. Are you feeling guilty as charged (karma catching up to you) or persecuted? *See* Judge; Jury.

CRAB

Crabs move sideways, avoiding the forward approach. This may indicate that you are side-stepping an issue. Or perhaps you are just *feeling crabby* today! It may relate to the zodiac sign of Cancer, the crab. If the crab is skirting the water, running along the edges of the sand, you are avoiding intimacy and the depth of emotions.

CRESCENT

Associated with the Goddess Isis, the new crescent moon heralds the return of the silver lunar light, a new beginning; waxing energy with promise and potential. An aspect of the Celtic Triple Goddess, a crescent represents the feminine in her maiden aspect. Associated with the Goddesses Persephone and Artemis. *See* Moon.

CROSS

In the Christian tradition, the cross represents the union of heaven and earth. In a dream it may symbolize the Christian religion, its tradition, or simply faith. For some, the cross epitomizes suffering and sacrifice. *See* Celtic Cross.

CROW

The shapeshifter and messenger, a crow is often familiar to the Witch, who relies on the crow's vision and warnings. Should you be more aware? Is there danger afoot? Listen to the crow and observe. Perhaps you have crow medicine, the ability to transport your thoughts and intentions, to shapeshift or heal from a distance. *See* Raven.

CROWN

A sign of royalty, privilege, and leadership, a crown is like a halo of gold around the head, open at the top, in order for the person wearing it to remain open to receiving divine guidance. Have you accomplished a great task lately, a huge achievement, your crowning glory? Look at tarot court cards and see if you can recognize yourself in one of them. Meditate on the meaning. *See* Gold; Hat; Head; Chakras; Jewels; King; Queen.

CRYSTALS

Minerals from Mother Earth are believed to contain energy and healing powers, crystals are spiritual and full of magick. Pay attention to how they appear in your dream. Perhaps a specific crystal is being shown to you for a purpose. See appendix A and appendix B, where you will find information about correspondences and chakras. Your subconscious may be guiding you to heal yourself or someone else. *See* Jewelry.

CUP

A container, associated in tarot with the heart, emotions, tears, and blood. Is your cup full, running over? Or is it empty and in need of some renewing life-giving waters? Remember, you cannot continually pour yourself out to others without taking the time to refill your own cup. *See* Chalice; Drink.

CURTAINS

Drawing curtains can mean that you feel something is finished. Over. "It's curtains." Or it might be that you are shielding/hiding yourself, blocking out the outside light, not wanting to face the day (consciousness). Is the curtain like a veil, a thin divider between two worlds, two realities? *See* Veil.

DAGGER

A weapon easily concealed, a dagger may signify betrayal, the danger of being stabbed in the back. More positively, it may be a sacred Goddess tool, an athame, used in ritual, symbolizing the air element of mental clarity, cutting through space to separate the sacred from the mundane. *See* Air; Athame; Knife; Sword.

DAIMON

A subtle variation on the concept of the woman's Animus, her inner male guide, the Daimon Lover is a spiritual masculine presence in dreams and imagination, the internal pathfinder who inspires passion and creativity. Whereas an Animus may direct a woman's focus out into the external world, often giving her courage, strength, and access to her voice, the Daimon is the burn toward creativity, inspiring the woman to love, to express, to emanate passion from her very soul. He may appear as an elusive ghostly figure or a charismatic lover, depending upon the dreamer's relationship to her source of passion. A woman may unconsciously project her Daimon onto actual living men, searching for him outwardly. Who is the Daimon in your dream, and how is he responding to you? *See* Animus; Archetype; Lover.

DARK

Dark represents the unknown, that which has not been illuminated to us. It is associated with the unconscious and subconscious self, with going within, taking a soul journey, the dark night of the soul, and exploring the depths. Cocooning. Hibernating. A time apart from the consciousness of *doing,* darkness is more about *being. See* Night.

DARK GODDESS

See Madonna.

DAY

The light of day, daytime is consciousness, bringing things to light. The dawning of ideas, of opportunity. A new day. New beginnings. Possibility.

DEATH

A very complex symbol. What has died? A part of yourself? A phase or a role of your life? An old dream/aspiration? Is this dream death warning you that you are deadening your feelings? Has your innocence (a child) died? Or some aspect of your instinct? (An animal? If so, which animal?) It can also mean change, transformation. Letting the old die to get ready for the new. Meditate on the Death card in tarot. *See* Buried; Destruction; Killing; Skull; Violence.

DEER

A female creature, feminine instinct, gentleness. Magickal. A gift. Associated with fairies, the deep green woods. *See* Forest; Stag.

DESERT

A barren landscape, dry, parched. Lack of feeling. Emotionally dry and empty. Little sign of life. Stark reality. Of course, the desert can be absolutely beautiful, colorful, and is deceptively full of life forms.

What associations do you have with the desert? Do you feel deserted? Alone?

DESTRUCTION

Mass destruction could mean that you feel your life is a disaster, or soon will be. Are you in crisis? Perhaps it is warning you that certain behaviors or choices could lead to self-destruction. Think symbolically. *See* Accident; Nuclear War; War.

DEVIL

See Horned One/Horns.

DISEASE

Ill health. An aspect of yourself or your life is not healthy. Something needs attention and healing. Follow your intuition. If the dream is disturbing and specific to a part of your body, get it checked out. Our bodies are wise and can send us warnings. Pay attention. *See* Hospital; Medicine; Prescription.

DISKS

See Circle; Coins; Pentacles.

DOG

How do you feel about dogs? Are they loyal, faithful? Are you afraid of them, of being bitten? Dogs can be playful, rambunctious, messy, hungry, protective, fierce, or puppyish. Find the association that fits. This will give you a clue as to what aspect the dog represents to you.

DOOR

A new opportunity opening to you, a choice. A way into another awareness, another world. The future. Access to a new level of understanding. *See* Entry; Threshold.

DOVE

The dove is an age-old symbol for peace and gentleness. Connected with the spirit.

DOWN

Going down, below, is going beneath the surface, toward the sub-conscious, plumbing the depths. Or perhaps you are feeling down lately. Has something triggered depression? *See* Ladder; Stairs; Swimming.

DRAGON

A dragon can be a complex symbol, containing aspects of the four elements: flames (fire), wings (air), fish scales (water), and living in a dark cave (earth). A dragon is the primal force of life, paradoxical. In its containment of opposites, the dragon teaches us about our own dualities: light and dark, feminine and masculine, creative and destructive, inward and outward. In its power and primitive energy the dragon symbolizes this underlying, unifying force deep within us all. It is primal energy, archetypal and ancient. *See* Archetypes.

DRINK

You are drinking in, accepting, receiving something. Renewal, ful-fillment, new ideas, affection, love, admiration? What fills your cup today? *See* Alcohol; Cup; Chalice; Milk; Water; Wine.

DRIVING

If you are driving the car/truck, you are feeling in control of where you are headed in your life. You are making the decisions, you are at the wheel. If someone else is driving, you may feel that you are not in control, that the person driving represents some influence or control over your destiny, your future. What is driving you? *See* Road; Travel.

DROWNING

Immersion in water (emotions/subconscious) can mean feeling submerged in emotions, drowning in sorrow, engulfed in grief that feels overwhelming. If there is fear in the dream, you may be afraid that emotions may truly drown you. Or are you "drowning your sorrows" with self-medication, alcohol, or drugs? See Boat; Lake; Ocean; Water.

EAGLES

Soaring eagles are associated with the spirit. Higher perspective. Freedom and strength. They are connected to sun energy and courage. You are being prompted to rise up and see the bigger picture. Eagle feathers are holy symbols for healing, and given to those who are worthy. Do you have high spiritual aspirations? See Air; Flying; Sky.

EARS

Are you listening? Are you able to hear what is being said to you, or are you blocking it out, denying information? There very well may be something you simply don't want to hear. Or maybe something is not sounding right to you. Listen to your own inner voice; your intuition. See Hearing; Music.

EARTH

One of the four elements, earth is about being grounded, connected to the Mother Goddess, the earth itself. Do you *know* where you are? Are you centered? Gaia may be speaking to you. Earth can also be about the material aspect of life, the physical. Matter. Read up on the suit of Pentacles or Coins (Disks in tarot). They embody earth energy. See Cave; Field; Goddess; Landscape; Mother; Mountain.

EATING

Ingesting ideas, information, and experience. Assimilation. What is someone feeding you? Is it palatable to you, or do you want to reject it? Perhaps this is about someone/something nourishing you. What we take into our body has energy that becomes a part of us, our energy system. Is what you are eating nourishing or poisonous? Helpful or harmful? What are you swallowing (accepting)? *See* Drink; Food; Teeth; Tongue.

EGG

Potential. New life. Fertility. Conception. A new idea. Promise. You may be giving birth to something new. If you are keeping the eggs warm until they hatch, you are nurturing some new ideas or creative projects, getting ready to "hatch" a new beginning.

ELECTRICITY

Power. Charge. Energy. Is something shocking? Electrifying? You may be experiencing an intake of power, an increase in your abilities, a gathering of energy.

ELEPHANT

A beast of enormous size. Is something in your life growing in proportion? Can you handle it? Is something or someone taking up a lot of psychic space? Elephants are often associated with memory, as well.

ENTRY

Entering into new territory or awareness. Is the entry into a room or a structure, a new aspect of the self? Or the basement, your subconscious? If you have the key, you hold the ability to access this next phase. If the entry is locked, you fear that this new knowledge or growth is inaccessible to you. If something stands in the way of your entry, you feel an inner block, an obstacle is holding you back.

Think about how you can overcome this inner obstacle. *See* Door; Lock; Key; Threshold.

ESCAPE

Do you need to escape a bad or threatening situation? Or are you avoiding facing an issue, running from the truth? Are you feeling trapped in a situation and long to be free? *See* Running.

EVERGREEN

A tree of hope, the evergreens remain verdant throughout the long gray winter, reminding us of the life that will return in the spring, a sign for us that the Goddess is, indeed, still green, still alive, eternal. *See* Goddess; Green; Tree.

EXPLOSION

Explosions in dreams can be powerful and positive, signaling a major breakthrough in awareness, or the expression of repressed emotions, anger, or rage, exploding into consciousness. The breaking up of old patterns or defenses. Major change. *See* Fire; Volcano.

EYES

Vision; one of the five senses; seeing. An eye can be an all-knowing presence, such as a God or Goddess. The universal mind. Eyes are also the "windows to the soul." Are you seeing something clearly? Are you not seeing the truth? Are you closing your eyes to something? Is someone looking right through you? Can you believe your eyes?

FAIRY

From Celtic lore, fairies are magickal creatures that live in the realm of the nature spirits and sprites. It is believed that fairies can be quite mischievous with mortals, playing tricks on them and luring them away from their safe abodes into the twilight world of in-between.

Do you have a fairy in your life? A part of yourself may be causing you some interior mischief. Playing tricks. Often an aspect of our inner self will trip us up and cause us to behave foolishly. It's a humbling experience for the ego. In Native American lore the role of the archetypal Trickster is played by Kokopeli and Coyote.

FAILING

Are you failing an exam? Not passing the test? Anxiety about failure may mean a tendency toward perfectionism. Perhaps you feel as if the collective is grading your performance, judging your standards. Yet, your own inner critic can be the harshest judge of all.

FALCON

Falcons are hunting birds, associated with hawks. They are fast and deadly. Is the falcon your own hunting instinct? Falcons are trained, hooded by trainers in order to control and tame them. Is this the aspect you relate to? Being owned, trained, and hooded from seeing, from flying away at your own will? Is this about your killer instinct being hooded? (Domesticated?)

FALLING

A common dream experience, falling can signify a sense of losing one's foothold, footing, security. Anxiety about losing your position or status, or feeling threatened by a sudden change or loss (such as divorce or death of a loved one) can trigger a falling image. Or do you feel as if you are slipping, losing ground, falling behind? Maybe you are falling in love.

FATHER

Dreaming of one's own father can be a symbol of your internalized parent. In other words, it may not be a dream about your actual father, but more about his attitudes, his values, how he dealt with the world, what he instilled in *you*. As we grow and mature, we internalize the values and standards of our parents, taking what fits us and discarding what doesn't. Your father may appear in a dream to show you a point of view, or remind you of the "family values" and codes he imparted to you. Do they suit you? Or are you fighting to break free of them and create your own set of values?

A father can also symbolize needing to seek the supportive, wise counsel of a fatherly figure. Reconnecting to our ancestors, the grandfather of wisdom, the paternal instinct. If negative, perhaps you are feeling the critical condescending judgment of a paternal viewpoint based on power, if not from within your own inner self, perhaps from someone in your life, or the collective at large. This is a complex symbol, and one that needs careful consideration based on your individual experience. The Emperor card in tarot represents the father, the paternal. *See* Archetypes.

FEAR

Fearful dreams feel intense and worrisome. Remember that it is a symbol, perhaps showing us our hesitations and fears about aspects of ourselves, our behaviors, addictions, defenses; most often the things that we prefer not to look at in our waking life. When experiencing a fearful dream, try to let the dream continue, allowing it to show you what you are afraid of. Facing our fears is a big step toward internalizing our true power. Work with the fear in chapter 7, A Witch's Dream Tools.

FEATHER

Symbolizing the air element, wings, birds, flight, travel, ideas, and messages, feathers can be signs given to us in nature, often guiding us in our searching. Note the size and color, and the specific bird that you think the feather came from. The meaning will be enhanced, linking the bird's symbolism to the feather in your dream. Receiving a feather may symbolize you have been chosen as an apprentice to learn the mysteries. *See* Birds; Flying; Wings.

FENCE

A boundary, a limit, protection, or division, a fence can mean different things, depending upon the connotation in your experience. Think about your own associations to the concept of fence. Are you feeling fenced in? Or do you need to set up some boundaries in your life?

FEMALE

See Anima; Muse; Shadow.

FIELD

The land is the Mother Earth, the Goddess, and her fields are full of life and nourishment, flowers and grasses. Often in dreams and shamanic journeying we find ourselves in a field, the wind is in our hair, the open space and beauty of earth fills us with peace. This is a safe place, a return to our Mother Goddess, a longing for reconnection to the earth. *See* Earth; Flowers; Goddess; Landscape; Weather.

FIGHTING

Usually fighting indicates conflict or opposition. Are you engaged in a battle of some sort? Are you experiencing conflict, inner or outer? Are you your own worst enemy? *See* Violence; War.

FIND

Self-discovery, finding something within you that you had not known or recognized before.

FIRE

One of the four elements, a deeper exploration of the meaning is explored in appendix A. Fire is a rich symbol, signifying many things, from heated emotions like anger to burning passions and inspiration. It can signify transformation, purification, desire, or destruction. The intensity of fire is a clue to how it fits in your dream. Think about word play as well, such as getting burned or burning desire, being fired or fired up. Hot, heated emotions are often the cause of fire dreams. *See* Alchemy; Candle; Cooking; Hearth; Explosion.

FISH

Dreaming of fish is usually indicative of spirituality. Fish swimming in water (the subconscious) can be messages or spiritual impulses, knowledge. Aspects of our subconscious self. *See* Fishing; Lake; Ocean; River; Water.

FISHING

Fishing is an age-old symbolic practice of seeking, learning patience. Searching for knowledge or spiritual food. Plumbing the depths of our subconscious waters to find spiritual nourishment, purpose, and answers. *See* Fish; Lake; Ocean; River; Water.

FIXING

See Repair.

FLOATING

Floating in calm peaceful waters can be a beautiful dream experience, feeling buoyed by the depth of the subconscious beneath us, at peace with ourselves and our emotions. Riding the soft waves of our intuition. Going with the flow. Floating on air may indicate you are feeling ungrounded, as if you are drifting, without purpose. Perhaps you are journeying in your sleep, traveling without encumbrance? *See* Lake; River; Swimming; Water.

FLOOD

Overwhelming emotions and swelling overspill from the subconscious depths can prompt a flooding dream. Unexpressed emotions or repressed responses can bottle up inside and threaten to break forth in a washing flood. Are you feeling overwhelmed? Have you been suppressing your true feelings in a situation? Begin to let some of your feelings flow, before they truly overwhelm you. Writing in a journal is an excellent outlet. *See* Boat; Landscape; River; Water; Weather.

FLOWER

Flowers are linked to the feminine, to sensuality, beauty, and sexuality. Some particular flowers are spiritual symbols. Roses are feminine, love, and sexuality. *See* Lily; Lotus.

FLUTE

A musical instrument, linked to enchantment. Mythic figures such as Pan, Kokopeli, and Krishna used the magic of sweet music to lure others to join them in dance, sexual revelry, or mischief. *See* Coyote; Trickster.

FLYING

Flying through the air, above neighborhoods and streets, fields and mountains can be an exhilarating dream experience. Have you risen above something? Have you been set free? Flying can be a spiritual exaltation, an expression of psychic agility. Freedom of movement and thought. Traveling through alternative awareness. It can also mean not feeling grounded. If the flying is unpleasant or dizzying, perhaps you need to ground yourself. Or are you avoiding responsibility by flying away, preferring to escape the burdens of responsibility through flight, à la Peter Pan? *See* Airplane; Airport.

FOOD

Taking in food can be symbolic of nourishing yourself. Or receiving and ingesting ideas, knowledge, food for thought. Chewing on issues or problem-solving. If someone is dishing out food that you dislike or despise, is this about having to swallow someone else's ideas, control, or values that are unappetizing to you? Something you just can't stomach? On the bright side, food is also pleasure, and sharing food is indicative of the ability to share in the sensuality of life. Feasting is celebrating and accepting abundance. *See* Bread; Cake; Cooking; Fruit; Kitchen; Milk; Wine.

FOOL

The primary archetype of the Fool, just on the outskirts of civilization (the collective), has always been with us. He is the pilgrim, the unwitting wise one. The Fool represents our unconscious self, naive, simple, gullible. To begin the journey toward enlightenment and integration of self, one must first become the fool, seeing things from the outside, detached, childlike, and trusting. (If we were fully aware of just how difficult the seeker's path can be, we might choose not to quest at all!) *See* Archetype.

FOREST

A thick wooded forest can represent the unknown, either an unknown aspect of yourself or the unknown future possibilities, especially if it is dark and you feel a bit uncertain. The dark woods can be associated with childhood fairy tales, getting lost in the forest. Does the dream feel positive or negative? Examine your feelings about the imagery in the dream. Is this about you feeling a bit afraid of the unknown, or is it simply about exploring unfamiliar territory? For me, the woods hold mystery and magick, do you share this view? It may then be about your own magickal explorations.

FOUR

A universal number of balance and proportion, stability. A sacred number, as there are four seasons, four elements, four directions, four races (red, white, black, yellow) of humans, four quarters, four winds, and the human heart has four chambers.

Fox

Smart, sly, and able to blend in with their surroundings, foxes are indicative of the cunning animal instinct. Spiritually, as a guide, the fox may signify a need for you to use camouflage, to observe and be keen, patient. Think about how the animal appeared in your dream. What is the fox trying to teach you or warn you about?

Freezing

Frozen water may indicate the freezing of emotions, emotional coldness, an icy detached view. Or perhaps you are feeling frozen, stuck, static, unmoving. Caught and trapped by a situation that chills you to the core. Examine what is frozen, and this will give you a clue. *See* Ice; Snow; Water; Weather.

Frog

Thanks to fairy tales, frogs and toads are part of the collective's image of Witches with their bubbling cauldrons of reptilian ingredients. How was the frog appearing in *your* dream? In Native American symbology, the frog is associated with water; his song is believed to bring the rain. Was the frog singing in your dream? Do you need to bring cleansing rains forth, or do you have childhood associations with frogs that will help you find a correlation? Did the frog in your dream ask for a kiss, as in the famous fairy tale? If so, there may be a prince in your midst that you're not recognizing!

Fruit

Fruits represent pleasure, sensuality, and nourishment. We associate fruits with paradise and gardens, Eve and Aphrodite. Also sexuality, with evocative fruits such as figs and peaches. Pomegranates are associated with the Goddess Persephone, who ate only its seeds during her underworld stay with Hades. Grapes connote pleasure, wine, and the God Dionysos. Tomatoes (yes, they are a fruit!) are linked to love. Apples (their core containing the five-pointed star) are a favored fruit of the Goddess, signifying wisdom and immortality. *See* individual fruits; Goddess.

GAME

Perhaps someone is playing games with you. Or are you treating life as a game? Do you feel as if someone is keeping score and imposing rules? Is the game fun, or frustrating? Examine whether you are a willing participant, or a spectator on the sidelines. Do you long to join in, get in the game, and feel you cannot? Maybe you feel that someone in your life is not taking you seriously.

GARBAGE

Indicative of the old, the outworn and discarded, accumulated left-over debris can mean it's time to clean house, clear out your mind, get rid of unwanted and rejected aspects of yourself, your life. Are things piling up? It may be time to simplify. Garbage is waste, perhaps you are wasting energy, time, or effort.

GARDEN

A place of the spirit, a reflection of the soul, a garden in bloom is inner beauty and possibility, growth and fruition. A tired garden full of weeds means you need to take some time and tend to your soul's growth. Nurture and fertilize, care for and invest. This garden is a reflection of you. If your garden is trampled, your spirit may be bruised by someone in your life situation. *See* Earth; Flowers; Landscape.

GATE/GATEWAY

An entryway; a passage into another world, another awareness. A choice—to walk through or not. An opening to the next world, or a new phase in your life. *See* Door; Entry; Threshold.

GATHERING

Is the gathering a happy occasion, or a threatening crowd? The atmosphere of the situation will inform you just what this group of people is about. It may be a celebration, a reunion of like-minded souls. Often a group of people can symbolize the collective mind, the prevailing opinion and group values. Do you fit in here, or do you feel apart? What is your place in this gathering? If you are in the *act of gathering*, this is about researching or collecting, perhaps ideas, information, or spiritual knowledge. *See* Basket; Collective; Food; Garden; Group.

GHOST

Symbolizes the essence of someone once fully alive, accessible, and participating, but now gone. A ghost can be a memory, a recognition that spirit has departed from body (the concrete, matter), and the life force no longer thrives on the physical plane. Has the spirit or essence of something once vital departed? It could be a relationship, a marriage, a job, a project. On a practical, literal level, we Witches *have* been known to receive messages from the dearly departed. Have you seen a ghost lately?

GIFT

A present, a gift. Who is offering you something? Are you aware that this gift is being given to you? Are you acknowledging the situation that has presented you with this opportunity? Are you able to accept this offering?

GIRL

See Anima; Child.

GLASSES

Corrective lenses. Are you seeing things clearly? Do you need to correct your vision, your ability to see the situation, the person? If the glasses are broken, you have lost the ability to really see things clearly, as they truly are. Your perception may be distorted.

GOAT

Associated with heights and climbing, goats can symbolize ascension, the tenacity required to attain a goal. Goats can also carry the collective projection of blame, become the sacrifice, as in scapegoat, symbolizing a victim mentality. Are you currently blaming another? Or do you play the role of victim yourself, accepting the projection of blame?

GOD

The divine masculine principle. The Great Mystery. The Lord. The beginning and the end. The Power. The Energy.

GODDESS

The divine feminine principle. The Great Mystery. The Lady. The beginning and the end. The Source. The Matter.

GOLD

An incorruptible precious yellow metal. Used for measuring value (the gold standard), gold is associated with the sun, masculine energy, and power. Was the gold in the form of jewelry, something costly (adornment, status, value)? This dream could be about your values, self-esteem, or the cost of such. Perhaps it represents that within you which remains incorruptible. See Alchemy; Clothes; Coins; Crown; Jewelry; Ring.

GORILLA

So human in many ways, gorillas are big beautiful beasts with heart. If you dream of a gorilla, I would venture to say that you are dreaming of your own wild self. The Wild Man archetype or the Wild Woman. Your inner untamed instinctual self. Get in touch with that part of you. It is lost to many.

GRAIL

The holy cup, sacred chalice. Searching for the Holy Grail is symbolic of searching for the lost part of yourself, the missing piece, the elusive dream, the ideal, the best part of you. Because it is a cup, a receptacle, the Grail is also feminine. I have always felt that the Grail symbolized the lost aspects of the Divine Feminine, that which we have lost in two thousand years of exalting the patriarchal values of dominion, expansion, intellect, status, and technology. The Grail could be the Mother Earth, Gaia herself. *See* Chalice; Cup; Drink; Goddess.

GRAVE

An aspect that is buried, laid to rest. A part of you no longer alive, or perhaps a relationship, an old wound, a painful memory. *See* Buried; Death; Landscape; Skull.

GREEN

The color of plants, herbs, our green earth, spring. Green symbolizes growth, new life, and healing. A Green Witch is one who concerns herself primarily with herbcraft, nature, trees, and working closely with the environment. Green is associated with the heart chakra, and loving beyond oneself.

GRIMOIRE

A magickal book of secrets, recipes, acquired knowledge. Also associated with the Book of Shadows, though the two can be separate. *See* Book.

GROUP

Depending upon the nature of the group (family, a team, a crowd, a mob, a class), this symbol may be about their collective influence upon your sense of self, your values, your individuality. Are you happy in this group, or longing to break free? Do you enjoy being part of a team, or prefer solitude? How do you fit in? This group, if it is a diverse bunch, may also represent various aspects of yourself. Sometimes it can get pretty crowded in there! *See* Collective.

GUN

A powerful weapon. The ability to cause immediate change and irreparable harm. Having swift impact. Do you need to make a change? Is the gun pointed at you? (Time is running out.) How can you accomplish this change?

HAIR

Associated with conscious thoughts. Hair grows out of the crown chakra, the gateway to higher awareness, the crown of the head. Hair also symbolizes power. The more the better. Is someone trying to cut your hair (take away your power or cut off your expression of ideas)? Put a lid on it? Or is your hair growing (increasing your power)? Is it changing color? (Look up the color listing.) *See* Head.

HALLWAY

A passage to another room or area. Houses and buildings are symbols of the self. A hall would indicate the pathway to another room, access to another awareness or aspect. If the hallway is brightly lit, you are conscious of this access. If the hall is dark, this is unexplored in your subconscious, unknown to your conscious mind. What is your emotion here? *See* Apartment; Building; Door; Entry; Home/House; Room; Stairs; Window.

HANGING

Are you hanging from a height, hanging on by the edge? Barely hanging on? Or are you the Hanged Man in tarot, forced by life to hang out for awhile, upside down, seeing the world from a different perspective, another viewpoint? With tenacity and patience we can learn to *hang in there* and learn another way of looking at our situation.

HAT

A head covering, hats might represent trying on a new identity or occupation, wearing a different hat. Or covering up your crown chakra, keeping your energy to yourself, hiding your thoughts. Keeping your ideas under your hat. What kind of hat is it? If you're wearing a baseball hat, that will have a different meaning than wearing, say, a nurse's cap. *See* Crown; Hair; Head.

HAWK

With his superlative vision, a hawk sees long distances. His ability to soar and observe from above gives him a broader perspective than ground animals. Perhaps you need to keep an eye out and watch a situation like a hawk. This could be a warning. Look out for danger, or even opportunity. The hawk is a predator and great hunter. Be watchful. *See* Bird.

HEAD

Dreaming of a head, yours, might be about your thinking, your brain, yourself as a thinking individual. Is someone messing with your head? Are you thinking clearly? If the head is disembodied, you are not connected to your heart, to life's physical, sensual experience. You may be getting too intellectual. Or are you losing your head? Think of word play: head's up, heading out, getting ahead. *See* Crown; Hair; Hat.

HEARING

One of the five senses, hearing symbolizes what we take in through the act of listening. What are you receiving or unable to hear? *See* Ears.

HEART

Emotions, compassion, feelings. Expression of love, empathy. Mercy. Is the heart healthy? Is the heart breaking? Longing? Heart's desire. Playing by heart. Heartfelt. The heart chakra is the gateway to the artistic impulse, creativity. The center of the body. Where suffering gives birth to compassion.

HEARTH

The sacred seat of the home, the home fires burning brightly. As the home is the self, the hearth represents its center, its heart. Its warmth. I once dreamt of taking my broom and dipping it into the hearth's glowing fire, calmly watching the flames glow on the end of the broom grasses. I felt warmed by this dream, heartened. As if I had a connection to all the sacred fires throughout time, touching the glow and brightness of faith in the Goddess. *See* Cauldron; Cooking; Home/House; Fire; Goddess; Kitchen.

HEIGHTS

Dreaming of high elevation can be about gaining a higher perspective on life, or feeling the sense of achievement, reaching the heights of one's powers or profession. If you feel fearful in the dream, you may feel a lack of foundation and support in your endeavors. You may feel at risk, as if you are attempting something beyond your reach, or exceeding your own expectations. *See* Abyss; Balcony; Climbing; Flying; Ladder; Mountain; Stairs; Tower.

HERMIT

The Hermit is an archetypal figure, a card in tarot. He represents the old wise one in the woods, the spiritual seeker, lonely on his solitary path. His spiritual rewards are wisdom gained through his seclusion. Profound isolation can bring a clarity of vision and purpose. Is the Hermit telling you that you need to take some time apart? To go inside your own self and seek advice within? *See* Cabin; Forest; Lamp.

HEIROPHANT

In tarot, the archetypal Pope, religious figurehead, keeper of traditional spiritual ways. He is more about the structure and even politics of *religion* than simple spirituality. Whereas the Hermit or monk in seclusion signifies the more personal spiritual path, the Heirophant is his opposite, regarded in society as a man of position and power. Often associated with judgment and inflexibility. *See* Priest.

HIGHWAY

Your journey in life. Are you traveling in the fast lane? Stuck in traffic? Racing by? Examine how you are moving on your life's path. What would you like to change?

HILL

Climbing a hill is working toward an achievement, a goal. If you have reached the top, you have succeeded! If you are slipping or coming upon obstacles, something is holding you back. You may feel that there are barriers to your attainment. *See* Climbing.

HOLE

If the hole is an "Alice Through the Looking Glass" kind of hole or passageway, you may be entering into another world, a different awareness. A hole can also be a dark place where things are hidden. Are you hiding something? Holes are empty. Are there holes or gaps in your life? Places to fill? (Let's not get Freudian now, shall we, dears?)

HOLLY

An evergreen, holly represents the male principle, and ivy the female. *See* Evergreen.

HOME/HOUSE

Your home is the symbol of yourself. The condition of it (well kept or disordered) may indicate how organized and integrated you feel. Are you comfortable in your home, happy with yourself? Or does it need improvement? Exploring a house can be exploring aspects of the self. Renovating and adding on to your house indicates growth and new psychic space. Putting in windows and letting in light is opening to consciousness and knowledge, illumination.

HONEY

A golden-sweet elixir, honey symbolizes fertility, as it is thought to be an aphrodisiac. The word *honeymoon* comes from the drink *mead,* which is made from fermented honey and was given to new-lyweds for one month to grace their lovemaking.

HOOD

Associated with hidden entities/forms such as death, messengers, and angels from mysterious realms. If this hood is covering you, what are you hiding? If a hooded figure approaches you, are you about to make a transition in your life, leaving behind the old to begin anew? *See* Death; Falcon; Hat; Head.

HORNED ONE/HORNS

In pre-Christian times, the Horned One was the archetypal masculine force of nature; he was fertility, the Great Stag, Herne, wild and powerful, effective, potent. The Horned One is the God principle, natural, associated with the life of the forest and the Green Man. Over time, through church propaganda his image was denigrated to representing the carnal (sensual = lust = sin) and evil, his great rack of horns morphing into the Christian icon of the horny red devil. For the record: There is no devil in pagan belief, Wicca, or witchcraft. *He is a Christian symbol.* If the Horned One has appeared in your dreams as the royal stag, or Herne, God with Horns, be glad. You are tapping into an ancient archetypal masculine energy.

If he appeared as the symbol of the Christian devil, examine your personal beliefs about your sexuality and sensuality. Are you struggling with the Christian collective's ideas about the body, pleasure, and sensual expression? Is the devil an embodiment of an evil force in your belief system? (Witches and Wiccans don't believe in an evil force.) The Devil may appear to those with a Christian/Muslim upbringing as a mirror projection of their own inner shadow. (He is an ever-present collective archetype in our patriarchal culture, after all.) If this is a shadow dream, you are facing your own self, your own devil, and your fears about the dark side of your own nature. *See* Archetypes; Shadow.

HORSE

As with other animals, horses can mean instinct. Strength, power, and endurance are also indicative of a horse's traits. The ability to get where you need to go. The means to move forward. Passion. Are you riding the horse, feeling the energy and force beneath you . . . or is the horse (your passion) out of control, wild and untamed? One dreamer I know dreamt of a headless horse, running fast and free. This could be about one's passions (sexual appetite), feeling out of control, and losing one's head (the thinking aspect) in the process.

HOSPITAL

A hospital is a place one goes to for something serious, major surgery (adjustment, corrective realignment) and repair. Does something need repair in your life? Do you need an attitude adjustment, or major psychological/emotional correction? Take the time to rethink things. And give yourself permission to heal.

HOTEL

Lodging that is just temporary. You are feeling as if you are not making a permanent commitment to something, someone. Your identity and sense of self may feel transitory. Or perhaps you just need to get away from responsibilities for awhile and gain a fresh perspective. *See* Building; Home/House.

HUNT/HUNTING

The primal urge to survive, the hunt is for survival. Attributed to the masculine orientation. Are you hunting down an answer, a goal, something for your very survival? Perhaps you are trying to locate a hidden aspect of yourself. Or are you hunting power? *See* Animal; Bow and Arrow; Deer; Forest; Jungle; Stag.

HUSBAND

Dreaming of a life partner can be symbolic of the marriage relationship itself, with clues like: who drives the car, (makes the decisions), who cleans house (caretakes), and so on, especially if you are aware of your specific Animus figure/Daimon Lover (masculine spirit) in your dreams. But a husband *may* indeed represent a woman's Animus, if the wife has unconsciously projected her own inner masculine onto her partner, expecting him to express it for her, rather than integrating the male aspect within her own self. Sound complicated? It can be. Examine your feelings within the dream. Did it feel as if this was about the dynamics of your relationship, your marriage? Or did it feel as if the husband figure was a mirror to your masculine self, your inner twin? Do you feel that you have a conscious relationship with your husband/partner? Or one full of projections and unconscious habits? *See* Animus; Daimon; Lover.

ICE

Frozen water (emotions) can be frozen response. Icy behavior. A cold heart. Or feeling stuck, frozen in time, in relationship. Without growth or signs of life. Frigid. *See* Freezing; Water; Weather.

INSTRUMENT

A means of self-expression, such as a musical instrument. If you are a dancer, your body is the instrument. It can also be a tool, an implement of change, alteration, fixing, creating, performing. A means to an end. Is this instrument yours? Did you craft it? Borrow it? Steal it? Or is someone offering you this instrument? Think about how you feel about the instrument in your dream, and how it is used by you.

INSECTS

Is something bugging you? Or are you displaying a trait of certain insects, such as the busyness of ants or bees (workaholic, self-sacrificing)? Spiders have connotations of the "Great Grandmother who weaved the world." Flies are pests and spread disease. Roaches inspire hatred and fear in many people. What was the context of the dream?

INVITE/INVITATION

Opportunity. What do you need, an engraved invitation?

ISLAND

Are you feeling isolated and off by yourself, unable to connect? Or are you longing to get away and spend some time alone with your own self?

IVY

An evergreen symbolizing the feminine principle, often paired with holly (the masculine principle). *See* Evergreen; Holly.

JACKAL

A negative animal symbol associated with scavenging dead bodies. Is there a part of you that is busy plundering the past, things that are dead and gone? Picking over what has died in you? Perhaps it's time to bury it and lay it to rest. In Egyptian lore, jackals led souls to the land of the dead. Let go of what needs to die within so that you may give birth to a new self.

JAGUAR

Powerful and sleek, jaguars are mysterious and mystical. Comfortable in the dark places. A familiar to South American healers, shamans, and Witches. If a jaguar visits you in a dream, pay attention! You are being called upon with great power.

JAIL

Are you locked in prison, held against your will? You may be feeling as if you are trapped in a situation, your freedom taken away. Or are you placing someone behind bars, some aspect of yourself that you are afraid to let out? *See* Cage; Lock; Key.

JEWELRY

Jewels and precious gems symbolize value, healing, and magickal energies. Are you being given jewels in the dream? (Precious spiritual gifts.) From who? Or are you finding them, like a found treasure? *See* Crystals; Gold; Silver.

JUDGE

A discriminating traditionalist, the judge may represent your own inner authority figure. When negative, this is the inner voice that fills your ear with judgments and criticisms. Or perhaps the judge is reminding you of your *own* judgmental attitude toward others. The judge may also represent societal collective disapproval, fed by your fears. Are you upholding the standard collective values (*their* law, *their* way), or are you guilty of trying to break free from the collective and stand your own ground? *See* Archetypes; Collective; Court.

JUNGLE

Our dream environment often clues us in on just where we're at emotionally. A jungle may represent our tangled wild untamed self. Our primitive urges. Or even paradise, depending upon your association with the concept of jungle. Analogous with rain forests, a jungle certainly is a powerful guise of the Great Mother Goddess, Gaia, in her rich fertility. Possibly a symbol for your fertile and rich subconscious. *See* Earth; Goddess; Green.

JURY

A jury of your peers judging you? This could be the power of the collective mind to influence you and pass judgment on who you are. Have you followed your own drumbeat? Do you feel pressure to conform? If the jury panel is various aspects of yourself, you may be judging your own behavior or choices, sensing the law of karma: What you send out returns to you. *See* Collective; Court; Judge.

KEY

Are you "holding the key"? Do you have the means to access what you need? Is something hidden away, locked from you, that you need to gain entry to? What is locked away? And how will you get to it? *See* Entry; Lock.

KILLING

As a dream symbol, killing can be indicative of killing off parts of oneself, one's past, aspects that are outworn and not needed any longer. Killing in a dream can mean that the dreamer understands the need to eliminate something from the self, for example: a habit, addiction, or dependency. If you are feeling anxiety or fear about the killing, look at the possibility that you have killed off some worthy aspect of yourself, such as your innocence, your openness to others (often symbolized by the death of a child, childhood innocence, trust). Think about the symbolic meaning of who or what is dead. You may need to resurrect it. *See* Death.

KING

An age-old archetype, reflected in myths, fairy tales, and tarot. The King is the figurehead, the father figure, the patriarch. Masculine power and divine authority. Look through the tarot Kings in their four suits and find which one may fit your dream image. Is it a positive image for you, showing you your inner strength and maturity? Or is it an oppressive figure who wields power over your life, your choices? See Archetypes; Crown; Father; Gold; Knight; Sword; Queen.

KISS

A coming together in a moment of affection, love, or passion, a kiss is communication and union. The desire to kiss, to love the other is a desire for wholeness and completion. Two opposites uniting, male and female, yin and yang, dark and light. A kiss is the start of the merger.

If you are kissing a member of the same sex, you are integrating other aspects of your identity, perhaps your shadow, unknown self. Or it could simply indicate self-acceptance. Less positively, if the kiss feels wrong or unwanted, it may be a warning of deceit. "Betrayed with a kiss." Be aware. See Daimon; Lover; Sex.

KITCHEN

The place within a house (the self) where ingredients are brought in (knowledge, ideas, thoughts, nourishment) and processed, transformed into food for the body and the soul. The kitchen is linked to the fire element, transformation. Cooking takes in raw material and transforms it into a palatable feast to feed the body and the spirit. This is your seat of alchemy! See Alchemy; Cooking; Eating; Food; Hearth; Home/House.

KNIFE

An aggressive symbol, a knife slices, cuts, and stabs. It is a tool and a weapon. Who has the knife in your dream? A knife can be a symbol of mental powers, clarity, the ability to cut through the bologna and get to the truth. Do you need such clarity? Or is the knife symbolic of a possible betrayal, being stabbed in the back? *See* Air; Athame; Dagger.

KNIGHT

A mythic archetypal figure in history, stories, and tarot, the Knight represents the ideal masculine—strong, selfless, and fighting for honor. Is the knight in your dream an aspect of you, able to stand up for what you believe in, championing others less fortunate? Or have you projected this ideal male image outward onto a man in your life? Are you desiring to be rescued by a Knight in Shining Armor who will whisk you away from responsibility? Are you facing a conflict and need to arm yourself for battle? *See* Archetypes; Armor; Battle; Grail; King; War.

KNOT

Representing the tangled complexity of life, working on a knot is problem-solving, requiring patience. Witches often do spellwork with knots, understanding the binding of energy and intention in making a knot. (Are you doing magick in your sleep?)

LAB

A laboratory is a place for experimenting, trying out ideas and theories. Are you doing just that? Are you experimenting in your life, or trying out various solutions to problems?

LABYRINTH

The symbol of the labyrinth has come to mean going within, finding a meditative state of being while following the curves of the labyrinth inward to the center, and then following the path out feeling renewed. It is about trust and patience. The spiraling journey within. *See* Maze; Path.

LADDER

Connecting below to above, a ladder is a means of getting from one such place to another. Are you going up into conscious thought? Getting higher in your perspective? Climbing the ladder of success or status? Or are you descending down into your subconscious mind, going into the undiscovered depths? Your ladder is the means to either transition. *See* Climbing; Down; Up.

LAKE

Water is the emotions. A large body of water can be the subconscious depths. A lake is usually calm, serene. The condition of the water and the nature of the lake can give you clues as to how your emotional life is doing. Calm? Or storm-tossed and turbulent? Is it clear and clean, or muddy and contaminated with pollution? Your lake reflects your state of mind. In Celtic/Anglo-Saxon myth, the Lady Of the Lake kept the sacred sword Excalibur safely hidden beneath the watery depths near Avalon. A clue for us on how to handle and reserve such power. *See* Sailing; Water.

LAMB

A young sheep, the lamb symbolizes innocence. Also think of the term *sacrificial lamb*. Is this about innocence and naiveté, or a sacrifice? *See* Sheep.

LAMP

Associated with consciousness and knowledge, a lamp illuminates our path, shedding light on our way toward wholeness, growth, and power. Often an Animus figure (the inner masculine) will carry a lantern for us, ahead of us on the darkened path, helping us to find our way. Accept his help. Any sort of knowledge—a book, a conversation, a sharing of experience, can light our way. So, keep the lamp light burning. *See* Hermit (as this tarot figure often carries a lantern); Animus; Candle; Light.

LANDSCAPE

The description of the landscape you find yourself in is a reflection of the territory you are existing in, the ground you walk on. Where are you? A dry barren desert with little life support or a lush green jungle? Think about your associations with this landscape and what it says about how you are feeling these days. *See* Desert; Earth; Field; Forest; Garden; Jungle; Ocean; Mountain; Snow; Weather; Yard.

LAUNDRY

Sorting laundry is a task of organization and sifting through accumulated components of your life. Washing dirty laundry is cleansing yourself, letting go and giving yourself permission to rebirth yourself, to present yourself as fresh and renewed. Taking care of the "dirty laundry" in life is not pleasant; we must often face the soiled aspects of our shadow selves, the side of us we'd rather not present to the world. Yet it is a task toward wholeness, and integrating all of our aspects. Everyone has dirty laundry. If you feel stuck with others' laundry in the dream, it may indicate that you are caught in the cycle of always having to clean up others' messes, being there to take care of others' dirt. See if you feel positive or negative about it in the dream. If negative, perhaps it indicates a tendency toward obsessive compulsive behaviors. *See* Washing.

LENS

A way to focus, an aid to see clearly. Is the lens distorted, fogged? Are you not able to see with clarity? *See* Eyes; Glasses.

LIBRARY

A collection of universal knowledge, a resource for understanding and wisdom. Are you longing for more knowledge, hungry for truth? Are you searching for meaning, for answers? What happens in your dream library? *See* Book.

LIGHT

Light is consciousness, illumination, spiritual truth. God and Goddess. The power of the universe. The sun's light symbolizes masculine energy, and the moon's light symbolizes feminine energy. Turning a light on can mean an idea or realization is close. *See* Candle; Fire; Lantern.

LIGHTNING

The flash of illumination, the surge of power, lightning is a potent dream experience. Are you on the verge of a great awakening to your power and potential? Has something triggered a flash of inspiration in you? In tarot, the Tower is struck by lightning and sudden transformation is foretold. Are you about to experience a swift unexpected change in your life or awareness? *See* Rain; Storm; Weather.

LILY

An age-old symbol of spirituality, the lily is one of the most beloved flowers. Its fragrance brings peace and opens the chakra centers of the body. Clearly, a lily in your dream is about awakening something spiritual in yourself. Is your spirit blooming? Lilies are also associated with the concept of resurrection in spring, rebirth. *See* Flower.

LION

In the law of the jungle, the lion is king. As an animal symbol, he is regal, powerful, and fierce. Are you in awe of lions? Or afraid of them? Your emotion in your dream will help you decide what aspect the lion is mirroring to you. Must you call upon some deep ferocious courage in the days to come? The lion will help you. Or do you feel you are being devoured by someone or some situation in your life? Turn to the lion in the dream and ask him what he has to tell you.

LOCK

Have you locked something away and tossed the key? Are you hiding something under lock and key? A fear, a secret, a desire, a dream? Are you trying to open the lock, to get access? Are you locked out? Or are you feeling locked into a situation that makes you unhappy? Perhaps you are longing for more security. *See* Key.

LOVER

To dream of a lover is to dream of yourself, the integration of your soul twin or opposite self. You desire the traits you perceive as opposite you. Making love in a dream is positive; you are loving an aspect of yourself, integrating your lover into a sense of wholeness, longing for the lost parts of yourself that you have discarded or never developed. You see these traits reflected back to you in the eyes of the beloved. See the listings for both Anima and Animus for a fuller explanation of our inner soul twin. When we fall in love we are desiring an aspect of ourselves to be recognized and integrated. The passion arising from encountering the dream lover infuses the dreamer with creative fire, an appetite for life and the desire to integrate aspiration into daily endeavors. *See* Daimon; Muse.

LUGGAGE

Are you packed and ready to move on? Have you lost your luggage (identity)? *See* Baggage.

MACHINE

Without soul, or Anima, a machine is merely the sum of its various parts. Are you feeling as if you are going through the motions, mechanically, with no love for what you are doing? No soul involvement? Like an Energizer Bunny repetitively going and going and going? It's time to stop and smell the roses.

MADONNA

A symbol of the divine feminine, the Holy Mother, Virgin Mary, Goddess of Blessings. A Black Madonna is symbolic of the dark feminine, the unknown Goddess aspect emerging within you. Dark because she is unknown, she is also the compassionate patroness of all who suffer, who know pain. She is the great comforter to those who seek her. Our Lady of Guadeloupe is one example of a Black Madonna. Sightings of the Virgin Mary have been increasing in the collective now for the past twenty years, indicating this rebirth of elevating the feminine ideal, the Virgin archetype. Remember that the actual meaning of virgin is *a woman complete unto herself*; not defined by her relationship to a man. Finding a Madonna in your dreams is a powerful archetypal experience. It is the energy of the Goddess herself rising within your consciousness.

MAGICIAN

In collective mythology, there is always a Magician, some figure on the outskirts familiar with esoteric mysteries, able to influence fate and outcome. This shaman or Medicine Man serves the people by providing them with access to other realities, helping them to become aware of the alternative worlds beneath the everyday surface. In tarot, the Magician supports you in discovering your own deeper powers, urging you along your sacred path. He is a mentor and a guide. If you are uncomfortable in your dream, or fear the Magician, look at the possibility that you may be deceiving yourself by your own slight-of-hand. Perhaps you are in the throes of *denial*, making something simply *disappear?*

MALE/MAN

See Animus; Daimon; Lover; Shadow.

MANDALA

Intricate designs in circular or geometric patterns that draw the viewer in as if in a labyrinth. Often used as a tool for meditation, many believe in the healing power of staring at a mandala. If you have one in your dream, you are perhaps approaching a new level of healing. A centered integrated sense of self. Or perhaps the mandala is prompting you to take more time to look inward and meditate, allowing your spirit to take your mind where it will.

MAP

The map of your life, the overall archetypal patterns that unfold before you. A guide, a scheme to help you chart your course. Do you have the right map? Or have you lost the map? Are you searching for a map? Feeling lost? Your dream will tell you where you stand.

MARKETPLACE

A communal place of exchange and commerce, opportunity. Perhaps the marketplace represents a range of choices to you, options, possibility. Are you browsing? Looking for something in particular in your life? A new identity, direction, or purpose? *See* Shopping.

MARRIAGE

Union. The merging of opposites. Two becomes one; integration. Vows and promises. Deep commitment. *See* Wedding.

MARY, VIRGIN

See Madonna.

MASK

Dreaming about a mask is symbolic of covering up your true self, showing a different face to the world, another persona. What are you hiding, and why? What mask are you presenting? *See* Costume.

Maze

Getting caught in a maze, unable to see the big picture is indicative of feeling lost, unsure of where to head next. Without the ability to rise above and see a more inclusive, wider perspective, we may lose our view of the forest for the trees. *See* Labyrinth; Path.

Medicine

Used for healing, medicine is magick, energy, and power. Are you taking a potion in your dream, drinking in healing energy? Or are you being healed by ritual, by a Medicine Woman or Medicine Man? Healing is taking place on a deep inner level. In western society, there is a belief that we must suffer medicine, such as the phrase "take your medicine." Associated in this respect more with karma, even a sense of punishment. The corrective impulse. Was your dream positive or negative? *See* Hospital; Prescription.

Milk

Milk is nurturing, the life-sustaining nectar from mother's breasts. Are you feeding, nourishing someone in your dream? (Nurturing an aspect of yourself?) Or are you drinking the milk, being fed, fostered? From what source? What nourishes you? *See* Breast; Mother.

Missing

Are you missing something, unable to grasp it? Have you lost something (your wallet: identity; money: values; keys: access)? Have you just missed your flight, your train, or bus? You are feeling like you have missed an opportunity. Do you feel left behind?

Model/Supermodel

The images of straw-thin supermodels assail us everyday from the covers of magazines, television ads, and movies. They are the products of our consumer culture, reflecting the *collective ideal* of beauty, the male projection of an immature, underdeveloped woman as an unbalanced society's Anima. If you are a woman and have dreamt of a model, the dream may be about your own struggle with the collective's concept of beauty and femininity. Do you measure up to the collective standard? (It is estimated that a mere 9 percent of our female population shares the physical traits of the supermodel. Does this mean the remaining 91 percent of women are undesirable? I think not.) A woman dreaming of any woman is dreaming of her own shadow, her denied aspects, her unknown and unacknowledged self. If the figure happens to be a supermodel, you might examine what part of your shadow relates to her. Do you have hidden issues with weight, food, perfection, your appearance? Are you accepting a man's projection of his Anima, living out this immature feminine aspect for him?

If you are a male dreaming of a model, you may very well be dreaming of your Anima, your muse, your projection of your ideal inner woman. Ironically, one of the top models is named Elle, which means *girl* in French, certainly appropriate for this culture's collective Anima figure: the less mature female. *See* Anima; Collective; Muse; Shadow.

MONEY

Money can symbolize our values, and how we take care of those values. What are our priorities? What holds worth to us? Have we lost our sense of values? Are we still searching for them? Are we exchanging valuable ideas with someone? Are we taking on someone else's values? Is this dream about self-worth? *See* Coins; Gold; Marketplace; Shopping; Silver; Wallet.

MONKEY

A monkey can symbolize a lack of control, addiction, an undisciplined mind. *See* Jungle.

MOON

Eternal symbol of the feminine aspect, reflecting to us her silver light. Her ever-changing phases represent the stages of a woman's life: the first crescent after the new moon is the young girl, the Maiden; the full moon in her completeness is a woman, Mother, pregnant with all her potential; as the moon wanes it reflects the surrender into the older years of the Crone; and the dark moon is death, going within, only to reemerge, reborn as the beautiful crescent, repeating the cycle of life, death, and rebirth. If you dream of the moon, note which phase the moon was at.

Examine how the moon's light affected you, and know that, indeed, the Goddess is alive and magick is afoot! *See* Goddess; Night; Star.

MOSS

I've actually dreamt of moss myself, grabbing onto it as I progressed up an ever-precipitous rocky trail. At first the meaning was a mystery to me, and I researched the symbolism to no avail. Weeks later (synchronicity at work), I read a passage in a book on Native medicine ways, and discovered that to certain tribes of American Indians, moss means ancient code, certainly apropos for my lifelong pursuit of symbology! *See* Forest; Green.

MOTHER

Dreaming of your own actual mother may not be about her in the outer real world. Your mother can represent your own inner parent. The mothering you received or didn't receive in childhood becomes an inner experience and takes on archetypal energy of its own. What you end up with is an internalized mother, a maternal viewpoint and value system that you absorbed from her. You can almost hear her voice in your own ear. If she was critical, she becomes the symbol for your own critical voice that jabbers inside your head. If she was loving, her love expands within you and you are able to give love to yourself and, hence, to others. You internalize her love. If you are struggling with accepting or rejecting the values she held, you may have conflictual dreams about your mother and your struggle to become a separate person. She is represented by the archetype of the Empress in tarot.

Dreaming of the Great Mother, or Gaia (such as a cave, a mountain, earth, a whale, a comforting breast), can be about your connection to Mother Earth energy. Mother is *mater* in Latin. The word from which *matter* evolved. How beautiful! Mother = Mater = Matter = Earth. Many women who have eating disorders and who are sensitive to food dream of the earth, of mother in various forms; the subconscious trying to show us the connection between how we value the earth, our mother, her ability to sustain us, and how food = energy. How we treat the earth collectively affects how we treat women's bodies. These issues run deep.

Mountain

Connected to the earth element, the mother, the mountain can evoke a sense of grandeur and peace, majesty and awe. If you are scaling the heights, this could be about your achievements, your progress toward a spiritual goal, an aspiration. *See* Climbing; Earth; Path.

Mouse

If your *cat* is dreaming about mice, it's all about dinner. For you, the dreamer, you'd have to think about your own associations to mice. Do you like them? Think they are adorable? Are you frightened of them? Disgusted? The mouse is associated with fear, having so many natural predators. One must also consider their caution as demonstrative of their survival mechanism. Are you receiving a cautionary message? To pay attention to detail, stay out of the way, and prepare for the future? Or is fear nibbling away at you? Have you been mousy lately? Your emotional response will clue you in the meaning of the dream.

MURDER/MURDERER

You may be feeling as if something or someone in your life is killing you, taking away your life energy or murdering your spirit. Are you dying inside? Is there an aspect of yourself that is killing you, such as an addiction, a destructive relationship, or self-destructive behavior? *See* Burglar; Death; Killing; Shadow.

MUSE

A woman, an angel, or feminine figure who appears in men's dreams and imagination as his inspiration. Reflecting an ideal beauty, she fuels his creativity by her mere presence, filling him with desire to express his passion. Linked to the concept of Anima, a muse is the inner feminine twin to a man's soul. He may unconsciously project this ideal onto an actual outer woman and look to her for inspiration, as in the classic archetypal tale of the poet Dante and his Beatrice. Ideally, he will integrate the muse into his inner self and feed his soul with her feminine viewpoint. *See* Anima; Lover; Model.

MUSHROOM

Grown in the dark places, mushrooms can be healing, magickal, or poisonous. Which kind was in your dream? Witches have always had knowledge of the growing things—herbs, plants, and mushrooms. This is part of the heritage. How is it manifesting in your life? Is the mushroom a symbol of healing, or mystery? Or some creative ideas that are busily sprouting in your dark subconscious? *See* Dark.

MUSIC

The language of the Gods, a nonverbal form of communication, inspiration, exaltation. Music can provoke emotions, even altered states of consciousness, trance. Musical vibrations are thought to be healing. Each of the seven chakras responds to seven different musical tones on the scale.

MUTE

A common dream experience: feeling mute, trying to cry out and no sound emerges. This is a frightening sensation. No one can hear you. You cannot speak. Are you speaking your truth in your life? Are you able to speak up, speak your mind? Do you feel *heard?* Meditate on your throat chakra and on *speaking* your truth. Wear turquoise around your neck. See Tongue.

NAKEDNESS

Whether being naked makes you feel exposed and vulnerable or simply skyclad and openly expressive, your personal feelings about it will clue you in to the meaning of baring all in your dream! All in all, it's about exposure, shedding inhibitions, or revealing your vulnerability.

NEEDLE

Using a needle and thread to sew things up, finish up, repair, or stitch (having to do with some unfinished business) can mean that you are taking control of the situation and following through. Getting the task done. If it's just the needle you are dreaming of, is someone or something needling you, poking you? If you are pricked by the needle (like the spindle prick in the fairy tale), drawing a drop of blood, this could mean sacrifice or initiation into the burden of a spiritual task that must be faced. A hypodermic needle may indicate desire to numb psychic pain. See Sewing.

NEGLECT

Is a child in your dream suffering from neglect? (Your inner creative spontaneous self?) Or someone else? Whoever or whatever is being neglected in your dream is an aspect of you or your life that you have been neglecting, not taking care of. See Orphan; Ragged.

NEST

Your home and place of safety and comfort. Do you have such a place, within and without? Or do you long for your own nest, your own cozy hideaway? Are you busy working on the nest, industriously assembling the bits and pieces necessary to create this place of safety? What are you constructing it with? Perhaps you are preparing to give birth, in actual life, or metaphorically with a new project. *See* Egg; Mother.

NET

Captured, caught, or being tangled in a net can be indicative of getting snarled in complications. Feeling tied up in knots. Snared in a web, perhaps psychological or emotional. Entangled in an uncomfortable situation. What is the web made of? How did you get into this position? *See* Knot.

NIGHT

Dreaming of the night is dreaming of darkness. Are you comfortable in the dark, the unknown? Can you navigate? Are you breezing through it? You are at home with your darker aspects, familiar with the cloak of night and the hoot of the night owl. The moon is your spiritual guide. Are you afraid of the lack of light, the shadows? This may mean that you are afraid to look at the darker unknown aspects of your inner self. In this case the night may represent being unaware. In the dark. Perhaps it is time to face some of the shadows in those dark corners. Ultimately, they are never as frightening as you fear. *See* Dark.

NIGHTMARE

I often think about nightmares as "wake-up calls." If we fail to learn the meaning of the messages that our subconscious sends us, preferring instead to ignore the more gentle nudges toward self-knowledge, then the subconscious has no choice but to get our attention, any way it can! Scary, startling images will wake us up, urging us to face our fears and shadows, prompting us to finally look at the issues that are simmering below the surface of our conscious mind. Jolting us out of complacency and denial.

Pay attention to nightmares and respect them. Give them consideration and they will reward you with revelations and insight. *See* Shadow.

NUCLEAR WAR

The ultimate disaster, nuclear war is an archetypal threat that may lurk within our collective unconscious mind for many years to come. If you dream of impending war, or an atom bomb going off, you may be filled with fear of the unknown and worry about possible disaster. You may lack faith in the common sense of humanity. Or on a personal level you may be feeling as if your whole world is blowing apart, changing irreparably, as through divorce or a death in the family. *See* Accident; Battle; War.

NUMBERS

Numbers are a universal language and have symbolic meanings and correlations often shared among different cultures. If a number is prominent in your dream, take some time to find what it may correspond to. Perhaps the numbered cards in tarot or the study of numerology. Check out the numbers in the houses of astrology that relate to issues of the self. Learn about the seven chakras, energy gateways to the body. Study the Kabbalah. There are *numerous* sources to go to.

OAK

A tree revered by the Celtic, Druids, and Norse peoples. The oak symbolizes deep inner strength, being rooted, grounded, and centered. The King of Trees, the Oak King, stands for durability and longevity, the primetime of summer and expansion. The God at his peak of power.

OBSERVER

Being the observer in a dream may indicate that you are con-sciously aware within your dreams of your subconscious self, mind-ful of the dream's message in an objective and open manner, able to understand the reality of your multiple dimensions. This aware-ness takes practice, but can be a rewarding experience, especially when facing some of the more fearful imagery. You can be calm and aware, standing firm, asking the dream image to tell you what the message is. On the other hand, it may indicate that you habitually detach yourself from direct experience.

OCEAN

Such a large body of water (emotions, life) is indicative of the vast depths of the subconscious mind. If the ocean is stormy, it may mean that you are feeling rocked by life's events, at the mercy of the raging sea. If you are sailing on smooth waters, you are navigating well and are at peace with your subconscious mind. Emotions are in their place and not threatening to you. If you are swimming, you are in the process of understanding what it all means, immersed and comfortable in the extent of all that awareness. If you are a woman swimming with a male partner, you are negotiating the depths just fine, in tandem with your masculine self, your Animus. Likewise, a man swimming with his inner woman, Anima, is doing the same, progressing with his feminine self.

Note: Whales are associated with the Goddess, ancient mother energy. Fish are spiritual thoughts and impulses. Turtles are also the Great Mother. The sea is rich with imagery and life, and reflects our deep knowing of our salty origins. *See* Sailing; Swimming; Water.

OCTOPUS

From the dark murky depths emerges an octopus. This multiple sucker-armed creature may reveal an entanglement, a clinging, unwanted involvement. Either that or you have a boss with some boundary issues who can't keep his or her roving hands still.

OFFICE

A place of work, profession. Is this about your professional self? Are you happy in your work, fulfilled? Do you need a change in your career? Are you bringing your work home? Examine your place in the office and make note of your feelings about it.

OIL

Historically, oil is precious, from olive oil to whale oil. It is a sacred substance, associated with ceremony and sanctification, initiation and ritual. Anointing and blessing, consecrating. When it is a fragrant bath oil, it is luxury and healing. Aromatherapy oils are potent in magickal and healing properties. How was the oil used in your dream?

OLD

An old woman in a dream can be significant of the Crone and her well-seasoned wisdom, the hag and the Witch, the One Who Knows. An old man can be fatherly wisdom and patience, Father Time, the Grandfather, Medicine Man. Old and ancient places, buildings, and sites may represent your searching among the ruins, the remnants of the past. Looking for arcane knowledge. The wisdom of the ages. Is this search fruitful? Or, if it felt uncomfortable, like a warning, are you clinging to the old? Do you need to let go of the past and leave it behind?

ORANGE

The color orange is associated with autumn, the color of friendship and sharing, the harvest, pumpkins, and squash. Bounty. The fruit orange is juicy and refreshing, with an uplifting, happy fragrance. Which do you need, the color or the fruit? Orange is the color associated with the (second) lower abdomen chakra, the center for sexual energy, emotions, and creativity.

ORPHAN

A parentless child, an orphan in your dream may signify that a part of you has been abandoned and neglected. Look closely at the child. What traits do they possess? These very traits may be the ones you have left behind and rejected within yourself. Are you longing to reclaim them? Are you returning to this orphan to now make up for lost time? Do you need to ask forgiveness? *See* Archetypes; Child; Youth.

OUTER SPACE

The new frontier, space is limitless and cosmic. This may represent the universal cosmic mind, or flipped, as if in a mirror, the unlimited possibility *within* your self. In looking through a microscope, we see into the most minute detail of an unseen universe, smaller than we can imagine. It looks uncannily like outer space!

OWL

Oftentimes a familiar of the Witch, an owl represents clairvoyance and the ability to project oneself on the astral plane. Native Americans fear the hooting of an owl, as they believe that hearing it portends a death. An owl can be a symbol of wisdom, magickal arts, or deception. Owls are night hunters, silent and deadly, and have keen night vision. Perhaps your owl is warning you of a deception and to watch closely. If you have *owl magick* you may be drawn to the magickal arts. Resist using this powerful owl magick for the dark arts or impulses of the shadow. Think of Athena, the Greek Goddess, who used owls' wisdom to see the whole truth and speak it clearly.

PAINTING

Creating in the visual realm; bringing an idea from thought into being, into the framework of a vision; seeing; a painting. The process of originating an idea and bringing it into reality. The word *painting* is a noun (an object), and also a verb, the process of painting. If a color was prominent, look up its meaning.

PANTHER

A powerful predator in the cat/feline family, a black panther is a fierce spiritual ally. Sleek and silent, able to blend in with the night. Perhaps this animal is showing you how to handle a situation. With grace, silence, patience, keeping your power unto yourself until just the right moment.

PARALYSIS

Unable to move or react, feeling helpless. If you are dreaming of paralysis, examine how you are handling your life. Are you feeling absolutely powerless in some situation? Helpless? Unable to effect a change?

PATH

A clear symbol of your path: Where are you headed? Are you on the right path? Following your heart's desire? Are there obstacles in the way (boulders, stones, barriers)? *See* Climbing; Maze; Road.

PEACH

A sensual sweet fruit, the peach is about pleasure, sexuality. Living in the moment, enjoying sensuality, the gifts of the body, the gifts from the Goddess. *See* Fruit.

PEACOCK

Showy and eye-catching, with brilliant colored feathers, the peacock has various connotations within different cultures. Buddhists believe that the tail, with its multiple "eyes," symbolizes patient watchfulness.

Because of its obvious beauty, the expression strutting like a peacock has come to mean too much investment in the pride of one's appearance.

PEARL

Associated with wisdom and hidden knowledge. Grown within an oyster shell beneath the sea, this precious seed of wisdom lies below the surface of consciousness. Its soft sheen is reminiscent of the moon's light and, therefore, has feminine energy.

PENIS

The masculine principle, ability to penetrate; potency and power. If a woman dreams of having a penis she is becoming aware of her own inner masculine, her ability to penetrate the issues, assert herself. It may also mean creative potency, the capacity to create. Also, perhaps, a symbol of sexual identity. *See* Animus; Daimon; Lover; Sex.

PENTACLES/PENTAGRAM

The five-pointed star within a circle is a symbol of protection. The five points on the star represent the four elements, plus Spirit. A five-pointed star without the enclosing circle is often called the Witch's Star. Pentacles is also a suit in tarot representing the earth element; Pentacles and coins represent resource, exchange, the world. Study the suit of pentacles to learn the nuances of this arcane symbol, reflecting change, work, power, success and failure, gain. If there were a specific number of pentacle coins in your dream, look up that card in tarot. *See* Circle; Coins; Star; Witch.

PHOENIX

The mythic phoenix is half-pheasant, half-eagle, and perished in flames only to rise from the ashes three days later to fly again. The phoenix, therefore, symbolizes resurrection and rebirth, as well as the invincible spirit.

PHONE

Communication, talking things out. It may symbolize a kind of telepathy, communicating over distances.

PIG

Associated with the mud and the filth it wallows in, pigs are known for their stubbornness and greed. Is someone piggish in your life? Or have you been getting greedy, eating like a pig lately, or driven by mere compulsion? In contrast, some cultures elevate the pig and include it in celebration and feasting. Think about your emotional response to the pig in your dream.

PIPE

Smoking a pipe can be a sacred act when done with intention and a prayerful attitude. Sharing a pipe symbolizes making peace between individuals or nations. Let the smoke rise like prayers and communicate with the Spirit.

PLANET

A whole other world. Are you exploring new frontiers?

PLAZA

A central open space, perhaps symbolizing the center of your psyche, open to consciousness, daylight, and possibility.

POISON

What is poisoning you? An attitude, a fear, a prejudice, bitterness, or envy? Find the antidote: love.

POLICE

Guardians of the law, keepers of the peace. A police officer may represent your own inner discipline, moral standard. Are they helpful in the dream (protective, assisting), or are you frightened by their presence, anxious? (Feeling guilty? Or perhaps limited by their law and order, the collective's ideal?) *See* Collective.

POMEGRANATE

A fruit of the Goddess Persephone, whose eating of the seeds of a pomegranate obligated her to spend time in the dark underworld (symbolizing the subconscious). Perhaps the dream is telling you to take some time yourself now to go within, feed yourself spiritually. Conventionally, pomegranates have symbolized good health and longevity. *See* Fruit; Goddess.

PORCUPINE

A prickly fellow, the porcupine wears his defense out in the open for everyone to see. Do you need to guard your gentle nature with a few quills of your own? Or have you recently been stung by someone's defense mechanism? Spiritually, the porcupine teaches us trust.

PREGNANCY

Dreaming of being pregnant is a very positive dream. You are full with life and personifying potential, birth and new beginnings. Are you giving birth to a new phase of your growth, your life? A new project?

PRESCRIPTION

Permission to obtain medicine, access to healing. Linked to diagnosis. *See* Medicine.

PRICE

The cost of something. Is what you are considering worth the price you'll have to pay? Is the cost too high? Everything in life is an exchange of energy. *See* Coins; Marketplace; Money; Shopping.

PRIEST

A man of the cloth, a servant of God, spiritual leader. In paganism he is a representation of the divine masculine, the God principle. Was the priest giving you a blessing? If the priest in your dream is a traditional Christian, he may represent religion, based in a patriarchal tradition, often exclusive and condemning in nature. What was your emotion while facing him? Perhaps you are challenging tradition in your family or community. Questioning authority. A traditional priest acts as a go-between for humans and the divine. As Witches, we believe that the divine, the God and Goddess, exists in all things created, including ourselves. Divine energy is immanent. An intimidating thought for those who place themselves in the position of indispensable mediator. (They're out of a job!)

PRIESTESS

A follower of the Goddess, elevating feminine values and spirituality. The Priestess embodies the divine feminine, the Goddess mystery. The High Priestess archetype in tarot exemplifies intuition, knowledge, and psychic development. Dreaming of her might indicate that you are reaching a higher level of understanding, a deeper awareness of your spirituality, finding alignment with the ways of the Goddess. Trust your instincts.

PUNISHMENT

Associated with guilt and shame. Do you feel you need to be punished for something? Are you feeling like you are caught in a self-punishing cycle of shame and blame?

PUPPET

Someone else pulls the strings. Are you feeling in control of your life, your choices and actions? Or are you manipulating others, pulling their strings?

PURPLE

A spiritual color, associated with the crown chakra, the highest cosmic energy. It also connotes leadership and free thinking.

PURSE

A place to stash one's valuables, a purse contains evidence of your identity (wallet, identification, driver's license, and so on), credibility (credit cards), values (money, currency), and personal effects (power). A lot of psychic connection goes into your purse. Did you lose it in your dream? Are you searching for it? What have you lost in yourself? Is your purse overcrowded, disorganized (a reflection of your state of mind)? Think about how it reflects who you are. *See* Coins; Money; Wallet.

PUZZLE

Trying to fit the pieces together? A puzzle is about life's complexities. Alternatively, it can be a part of ourselves we are puzzling over. Trying to get all of our inner pieces to fit.

QUEEN

The archetypal Queen, symbolic of the strong and mature feminine. Representing our qualities of character, she is grace under pressure, fair, compassionate, strong, and insightful. The shadow side of the Queen can be jealous, worried, envious, and vengeful. Take out the four Queen cards in the suits of tarot and look them over. Does one speak to you? Read the correspondence. Do you have such a Queen in your life? Or do *you* want to be Queen for a day? *See* Anima; Archetype; Mother.

QUICKSAND

Sinking fast. Do you feel as if you have no support, no foundation? Perhaps you haven't planned ahead or made other options available to you. Is it time to examine your value system? What do you depend upon? On what do you base your truth?

QUILT

Stitching and piecing a quilt together out of various materials can represent your desire to integrate and bring together all the various aspects of your life into one whole. If you are snuggling under such a quilt, you are secure and comfortable with all the pieces and feel as if things have come together for you. *See* Puzzle; Sewing.

RABBIT

A sacred animal of the Goddess, the hare, or rabbit, symbolizes fertility. Being associated with the spring Goddess Eostre, the hare gave birth to an egg, therefore symbolizing rebirth. The tentative fearful nature of the rabbit can also be symbolic of your own fears and inhibitions.

RACE

Are you running in a race? The rat race? Are you racing with the clock, running out of time? Are you feeling the pressure of competition or longing to follow your own path? Or are you dreaming about your status, your place in winning the race? *See* Clock; Collective; Game; Path; Running.

RADIO

Broadcasting and receiving, a radio can be indicative of mental telepathy, energy vibrations, picking up on unspoken thoughts. Are you reading (someone) loud and clear?

RAGGED

Worn out, uncared for, disheveled, unorganized, outgrown, neglected. What aspect of yourself, or your life, is in rags? *See* Clothes; Orphan; Neglected.

RAIN

Water, emotions, sorrow, and grief. Tears. Rain is also healing, nurturing, and life-giving, a moment of grace upon the earth. A gift from the Gods above. A deluge of rain may symbolize the need to cleanse, clear out, and start over. *See* Storm; Washing; Water; Weather.

RAINBOW

Symbolizing hope, the eternal, diversity, a divine gift. The rainbow is a sign of promise and dreams being fulfilled. *See* Rain; Sky; Weather.

RAPE

A violation, intrusion, violence against your body (self) and soul. This powerful archetypal experience is devastating. Examine your life carefully. Perhaps you are being violated on a deep level that you are unwilling to face. *See* Violence.

RAT

Many negative connotations are associated with a rat. Hiding in dark filthy places, rats often disgust people. What is your reaction? What is the vermin doing in your dream? It may be about facing some of your own inner fears, or warning you that someone in your life should not be trusted. They may be a rat. Or maybe you feel caught up in the rat race and need to slow your life down a little. Laboratory rats are confined and experimented upon. Do you relate to such a predicament?

RAVEN

Raven magick is powerful, connected with the night, messages, and the mystical. A raven imparts courage in the dark places and a willingness to navigate the unknown. *See* Bird; Crow.

RED

A color suggesting emotions, fiery passions, heat. Seeing red means anger. Red is also courage. Examine what was red in your dream. For instance, a dreamer I know dreamt of a red bedspread covering her double bed (marriage). A fitting symbol revealing that her anger at her husband was a "cover-up" for a marriage filled with problems she was unwilling to face.

RENOVATE

Knocking out walls and renovating a house is symbolic of breaking out of the old self and constructing new aspects, new psychic space and inner growth. If you are adding windows, bringing in more light, you are becoming more conscious. *See* Building; Home/House; Stairs; Wall; Window.

REPAIR

Depending upon what it is you are repairing, the dream can mean that you are going within to restore and repair an aspect of yourself that has been injured, damaged, hurt, or impaired in some way. A positive dream indicating that you are taking responsibility to address an issue and rectify it.

RESCUE

What needs rescuing? A part of yourself that you've been denying? Examine who is doing the rescuing. It may help you determine where you need to go to find that which might save you. A young dreamer I talked to dreamt that he was drowning, and then was rescued, pulled out of the water by a famous artist in the music business. It turns out that this dreamer had hidden aspirations of being involved in the music scene. This dream illustrated that the dreamer felt he was desperately floundering, but his love of music and the choice to pursue it could virtually *save his life*.

RESTRICTION

Look closely at the restriction in your dream. Is it self-imposed? Are you literally holding yourself back? If not, what is?

RING

A ring is round, a never-ending circle, a classic symbol of the self. Are you wearing it? If so, what style is it? Egyptian, modern, medieval? Have you lost your ring? (Your sense of self?) Have you come upon a ring that fits perfectly? (Discovering a new sense of wholeness?) What metal is it . . . gold (masculine) or silver (feminine)? Does it have a stone? What color, shape? All these details will give you a clue as to how you value yourself. *See* Circle; Gold; Silver.

RIVER

An ancient symbol of life source and navigational systems. Rivers provide life-sustaining waters and the means to travel, connect with far off places. A river also divides land. Crossing a river can suggest that you are crossing over to a new territory, new ground. Perhaps you are ready to explore further the uncharted aspects of yourself. Being water, rivers can also be emotions, such as a river of tears. *See* Bridge; Landscape; Water; Weather.

ROAD

Suggesting perhaps where you are headed in life, the road you're on. The high road or the low road. The road less traveled or a congested highway. Is it a clear accessible road or a bumpy windy one? Think about your description of it. It may help you determine where you are headed and how you'll get there. *See* Down; Driving; Landscape; Running; Up.

ROBE

Clothing, a covering. A robe represents our outer persona, our image. Is the robe rich and luxurious? Is it ceremonial (indicating an initiation)? What are you covering up? How does the robe feel in the dream. Welcoming and comfortable? Secure? Thin and unable to keep out the cold? (Do you need more protection?) *See* Clothes.

ROOM

A room is an aspect of your inner self.

ROSE

Long associated with the Goddess Aphrodite, Star of the Sea, the rose became the symbol for the Virgin Mary as well. Indicative of feminine beauty in its soft layers of petals and exquisite variety of colors.

RUN/RUNNING

If you are running *away* from someone or something in your dream, perhaps you are attempting to avoid confrontation or facing a problem head on. If you are running a *race*, you may feel that your life is going too fast, there is too much pressure on you to keep up the pace. If the running is exhilarating and enjoyable, you may have reached a point in your growth where you are feeling unrestricted and able to run free.

SACRIFICE

One of life's truths, sacrifice has long been an aspect of worship and ritual. Reflected in the turning of the *Wheel of the Year*, the observation that growth and life (flowers, herbs, leaves, the green, crops, animals, and so on) is followed by the harvest, the sacrifice, death, in order that the people survive. Life continues. The ongoing cycle of growth, death, and rebirth is an integral part of our collective knowing, and mirrored back to us in countless tales and myths. Is part of you requiring some sacrifice in order for the rest of you to grow? Does something in your life need to be sacrificed for the common good or for future growth? (For example, a dead marriage or unfulfilling job?) *See* Death; Scythe; Seasons; Wheel.

SAFE

A hideaway. A place to stash valuables, proof of identity, proof of worth, secrets. What are you protecting, hiding away?

SAILING

If you find yourself sailing on calm smooth waters, you are navigating life just fine. If the wind is whipping and wild you may be feeling tossed by the circumstances in life, threatened by the ferocity of the storm (emotions). Or perhaps you feel simply adrift at sea, lost for the time being, unable to get back to a sense of purpose. *See* Anchor; Boat; Lake; Ocean; Water; Waves.

SALMON

A sacred symbol of the Celts and the Pacific Northwest Indians, salmon signifies abundance, rich spiritual food, and sustenance. A part of the Fisher King myth, the too-hot salmon burns the impatient young knight Parsival, the pain initiating him into his longing search for the Grail. *See* Fish; Fishing.

SALT

Symbolic of the earth element, salt is necessary to survival. It is also a preservative and adds taste and flavor to foods. Are you trying to preserve something, or add a little flavor to your life? Salt is also strongly associated with purification, drawing out negativity. *See* Altar; Earth; Food; Tongue.

SCARRED

The injury leaves a scar, evidence of the wound inflicted and the healing that followed. Where is your scar, and how have you healed? Notice its location and correspondence to the body, chakras, or the five senses. *See* Wound.

SCHOOL

A place of learning, of assimilating new information, knowledge, and skills. Life is a classroom, my darlings, what are you learning today? *See* Collective; Failing.

SCISSORS

An implement able to cut. Do you need to separate yourself from something or someone? Are you cutting a tie that binds? Severing a relationship? Cutting the chord, moving toward independence? Cutting something unwanted out of your life?

SCYTHE

The symbol of the harvest, death, the sacrifice of the Grain God, cut down in order that the people might survive, the scythe is in the shape of the crescent moon, the waning symbol of the Crone, the autumnal time of the year. Life sacrifices to life in order to be reborn. A sacred tool of the Druids, used to cut the mistletoe. *See* Sacrifice.

SEASONS

The four seasons represent the four stages of growth and life. Spring is fresh, the new beginning, renewed development, youth and green. Summer is maturity, fullness and expansive potential realized, ripening. Autumn brings the harvest, the ending of the growth cycle, moving inward, aging. The winter brings the cessation of growth, increasing darkness, the time of death, introspection and hibernation. All the while the roots and seeds from last year are waiting, dormant, yet potent within the soil, to begin the push of new life again in the spring. The wheel of life, death, and rebirth once again reveals to us the wisdom in nature's cyclic journey. Learn to tune in to the changing seasons and honor each phase by integrating each season's lessons. *See* Wheel.

SEED

The germ of an idea, the potential for life, a new project, a new aspect. Planting seeds may indicate that you are starting some new undertakings, intentions, thoughts, beginnings. *See* Wheel.

SELF

Being aware of one's self in a dream reveals an ability to pull back and objectively view one's ego. Becoming an observer can be a liberating experience. *See* Observer.

SERPENT

See Snake.

SEX

Desire toward union, the pull toward integration, sex suggests the urge to synthesize various aspects of the self, to pull together opposites or take in a new perspective into one's awareness. The person you are having sex with represents a specific quality that you recognize and desire to bring into your own awareness. Spend some time thinking about the qualities of the lover you desire in your dream. What you are attracted to is the very thing you need to develop within yourself. *See* Anima; Animus; Daimon; Lover.

SHADOW

The shadow is the unrecognized, denied, rejected, or undeveloped part of yourself that lives in your subconscious. She (if you are female) or he (if you are male) may show up in dreams as an actual shadowy figure, dark, perhaps half hidden, obscured in some way—threatening. The more unconscious (unacknowledging) you remain about your shadow, the darker and more frightening the figure will be. Sometimes you might see the shadow reflected back to you in a dream mirror. A common experience is a dream of gazing at one's face in a mirror, only to have it begin morphing into some monstrous or hideous guise. Your subconscious is letting you in on a secret: The shadow lives within us all. Once you accept that as a human being you share the potential of being *capable* of the *full* range of human emotion and experience (not only the good, kind and light impulses, but darker impulses as well), you will find freedom for true compassion and empathy within. Shadow dreams let us know where our own darker impulses lie, whether it be in the form of jealousy, rage, cruelty, and so on. If we can come to accept our shadow as a part of being human, we begin to make our daily choices on a more conscious level. Befriending our shadow actually frees up tremendous amounts of creative energy. This is a long process, and usually undertaken toward midlife, when denial of the shadow begins to drain one's energy and zap one's strength. After doing shadow work for awhile, you will find your dream shadow transformed into a companion, someone of your own sex who will accompany you on your night journeys, even assist you in exploring or problem-solving. If you refuse to acknowledge the shadow in your life, you can be sure that eventually it will erupt in startling unconscious behavior that will leave you stunned, shaking your head. For further insight into the importance of this inner aspect, see chapter 4, The Importance of Shadow Work.

SHAMAN

The role of the shaman is a sacred one: to access other worlds, to journey betwixt realities in order to find healing. If a shaman appears in your dream, you have encountered the archetype within yourself. Listen and follow. This is the aspect of yourself that has access to ancient knowledge and healing. The shaman may be your spiritual guide. *See* Archetypes.

SHEEP

A gentle nonassertive animal that has often symbolized the instinct to follow. Have you been going along with the crowd lately, not taking care of yourself as a separate individual, influenced too much by others?

SHOE

Dreaming of shoes may reveal an aspect of your identity. Notice the style and type of shoe. For example, a ballerina's satin-toe shoe would symbolize one thing, a rugged work boot quite another. Does the shoe fit? Is the dream asking you to reevaluate your identity or position, or try on a new personality, career? *See* Clothes.

SIGHT

One of the five senses, dreaming about sight may indicate a question about your ability to see something clearly. Or perhaps your subconscious wants you to look at something. Have you lost your focus? Can you see your way through? *See* Eyes; Lens.

SILVER

The soft reflected sheen of silver is reminiscent of moonlight, causing it to be regarded as the feminine metal, as opposed to the masculine gold. It is thought that silver absorbs light and energy. Polishing silver is symbolic of refining one's soul.

SISTER

Dreaming of a sister, if you are a woman, can be dreaming about an aspect of yourself that your sister reflects back to you, especially shadow aspects, the unflattering parts of yourself that you might prefer to keep hidden away. If a man dreams of a sister, it may represent his Anima, a twin soul, the feminine side of himself, an ally. Certainly, a woman can dream of a sister ally as well, an ally born out of the integration of her shadow self. *See* Anima; Shadow.

SKATING

A way of moving forward, transport. Skating may represent your ability to move quickly and smoothly through life, under your own power. If you are trying to skate on stairs or ladders, however, you are wearing the wrong footwear! Question yourself about how you are moving toward your goals.

SKELETON

An archaic symbol of death, the skeleton reminds us of our tran-
sience, our limitations, our inevitable end. If a skeleton appears in
your dream, you may be facing some kind of ending, or it could be a
reminder of your mortality. Perhaps the skeleton is showing you the
bare bones of something? It has no flesh and blood. Only the underlying structure. See Bones; Buried; Death; Grave; Skull.

SKULL

Read the entry for *skeleton*, yet also think about the fact that it's
only a head, a skull. Conceivably, it could be about a lack of soul,
for there is no mind, no soul in an empty skull. Only the shell,
made of bone. A void. It may mean a death, symbolically, or an
awareness of your mortality. See Death; Skeleton.

SKUNK

The animal renowned for and identified with its defense mechanism: that smell! Skunks are nocturnal and really cause trouble
when they want to. Is there a stinker in your life, or have *you* been
one lately? Does your reputation precede you?

SKY

The heavenly blue dome above, the sky inspires dreams, poems and
prayers, and thoughts of the world beyond, as it appears endless and,
with its horizon, full of possibility. Connected with the element of
air, the sky, air, and wind can symbolize mental action, clarity, and
purpose. Divine inspiration and spirituality. Also intellect. See
Weather.

SLEEPING

If you dream of sleeping, you must ask yourself, *What am I unconscious of? How am I not "awake"? What am I avoiding?* Are you sleepwalking through your life, just going through the motions?

SMELL

One of the five senses, smell directly connects our brain to memories and impressions. Aroma is powerful and can induce the brain to release chemicals of healing and pleasure. A disagreeable odor can cause a strong negative reaction. Our emotions are unmistakably linked to smells.

SNAKE

The snake is indeed a complex symbol. When the serpent is biting its own tail, forming a symbolic circle, it represents the eternal cycle: life, death, and rebirth. In its shedding of its old skin, the snake again standardizes the concept of renewal, sloughing off the old, beginning anew. Snakes were sacred to the ancient Goddess, holding the meaning of earth wisdom. If you are busy gathering up snakes, you are collecting sources of arcane knowledge. If you are bitten by a serpent in a dream, you are being initiated. The bite is the moment of pain, initiation into the mysteries of life and death. You will survive the bite and be reborn to a new awareness. If there is great fear attached to the image of the snake in your dream, you must examine your personal feelings about these reptiles and think about what meaning you associate with snakes. Christian mythology has denigrated the serpent and given the once-honored snake a collectively bad rep for two thousand years.

SNOW

The whiteness of snow can be symbolic of purity, a clean fresh start. Snow is also frozen water (emotions) and may indicate the chilling of feelings, frigid response. Associated with winter, snow may signify the natural conclusion of a phase in your life cycle, the end of passion in a relationship, stasis. See Frozen; Ice; Landscape.

SOLDIERS

Associated with regimentation, order, conformity, force, and battle, soldiers can symbolize those aspects within ourselves. Are you being held captive by rigid beliefs? Dominated by some force, feeling pressured to fall in line, conform? Are you fighting an inner battle? *See* Army; Collective.

SOUP

Simmering soup is nourishment, comfort food, something that warms us in our lives. Are you stirring the soup, adding ingredients? This could be about mulling over ideas, adding elements to what nurtures you. Creating your own recipe for your life. Are you stewing over something that is bothering you? Is there something missing in your soup that you are searching for? Where might you find it? *See* Cauldron; Cooking; Hearth; Kitchen; Stove.

SPACESHIP

Spaceships have become powerful collective symbols for transport into the unknown, exploring the *last frontier.* Examine your feelings about the ship. Is it exciting, a new opportunity for you to explore something unknown and previously out of reach? Or is it frightening, representing something scary and alien to you, threatening? Does it reflect your hopes or your fears? *See* Outer Space.

SPIDER

To some, spiders are frightening, reflecting childhood fears or irrational dread. To others, spiders are benign, one of our many relatives in the natural kingdom. Clue in to your personal feelings about spiders. Are they something fearful? Or is she a sister helper who weaves her web and keeps a lookout. Is she warning you of danger? Or is the dream about the art of weaving the web? Are you patiently constructing something yourself, weaving the strands like the spider?

SPIRAL

A beloved symbol through the ages, the spiral is connected to the way of the Goddess, the path of the ancients, the Old Ways, the circuitous progress of nature. Life is not linear, but spiral, turning in circles (cycles), coming around again to return to itself. The eternal spiral dance. *See* Archetypes; Circle; Labyrinth; Wheel.

SQUARE

With four equal sides, a square represents stability. It can also be a box, static, an artifice where one feels stuck, with no movement or dynamic.

STAG

To pagans, the stag represents the masculine principle, the King of the Forest, regal, powerful, virile, potent. The wild natural masculine force. *See* Forest; Horned One/Horns.

STAR

Divine guidance, protection. Destiny. Good luck and success. *See* Pentacle/Pentagram.

STAIRS

A means to move upward or downward. Going up stairs would signify moving upward into a more conscious level of awareness, or pursuing higher aspirations toward consciousness. Going down would indicate a move inward, below, to the subconscious realm, exploring the darker unknown aspects of the self. *See* Down; Up.

STEALING

Have you stolen something that does not rightfully belong to you? An idea, a method, a right? Or has something been taken from you? Do you feel that something (or someone, or part of yourself) in your life is stealing your time, energy, affection?

STORM

Turbulent weather can often reflect your own inner storm. Is a tempest approaching in your dream? Is there some upsetting or unsettling event appearing in your life? Or are you right in the thick of it? Usually storms are representative of powerful emotional forces. *See* Ocean; Sky; Weather.

STOVE

The stove is a center for transformation, a heat and energy source that generates change, cooks and bakes that which we take in for nourishment. Are you cooking in the dream, preparing food for thought or assimilation? Transforming ideas and concepts into something palatable, even delicious? The stove is a place where alchemy takes place. What are you transforming in yourself? What ideas are you cooking up? *See* Cooking; Food; Hearth; Kitchen.

STRANGER

The archetypal stranger exemplifies an aspect of ourselves that remains unknown to us. Unfamiliar. Unconscious. Is the stranger threatening? Why? Is the person intriguing? Try and face strangers and welcome them. Strangers often portend change, something new afoot. *See* Burglar; Shadow.

STONES

The earth element, stones have weight, quiet strength, and vibration. Crystals and stones can contain healing energies and may carry messages for us from the earth. Think about the context of your dream to determine just what these traits of the stones represent to you. *See* Earth; Mountain; Path.

SUFFOCATE

Without the element of air we die, suffocate, unable to breathe. Spirit is breath. What is stifling your spirit in your life? Is someone or something smothering your very spirit? *See* Air; Murder/Murderer; Throat.

SUN

The sun is pure energy, fire, life, masculine expression, consciousness. *See* Day; God; Light.

SWAN

An imposing (swans are big!), beautiful, and elegant bird, swans are associated with poetry, music, seduction, and love.

SWIMMING

Immersion, movement through water (emotions or the underside), swimming can be very positive, signifying your progress with navigating your emotional depths. Are you staying afloat, capable? Or is it tough going, difficult to remain afloat in your swell of feelings?

SWORD

The mighty sword has been a powerful symbol through the ages. Associated with the power of thought and action, clarity of decision, and the ability to penetrate to the heart of the matter, swords represent our mental ability to do as such, to swiftly separate truth from fiction: to discern, to decide, to clarify. Was your dream sword an ally? A gift? A weapon? Did it wound you or free you? Meditate on the suit of swords in tarot, or visualize your sword and ask it for its meaning and how it can help you.

TEETH

I often hear people talk about losing their teeth in dreams. First, think about what your teeth allow you to do: bite and chew. Losing your ability to bite may mean you are feeling unable to be assertive, to feel effective, potent. Or perhaps in your dream you have bitten off more than you could chew? Taken on too much. Are you biting into life, able to take your share? Or have your teeth fallen out, leaving you feeling ineffective, as if you've lost your animal instinct? *See* Eating; Tongue.

THORN

Every rose has its thorn, the saying goes. The prick of pain, initiation into the mysteries of the Goddess, of life, of beauty; the illustration of opposites, the duality of nature, dark and light, feminine and masculine, giving and receiving, inward and outward. For some, the thorn symbolizes suffering, for others, initiation.

THRESHOLD

On the verge of a new beginning, a new entry into another realm, a higher level, a fresh start, a different awareness. Take a deep breath, and walk through! *See* Building; Door; Entry; Gateway; Room.

THROAT

Corresponding to the throat chakra, naturally, the energy center from which we speak our truth, the throat is where we find our voice and sing our song. Expressing who we are to the world. *See* Chakras; Tongue; Turquoise.

TOMB

A place of rest; a sacred place of keeping. The temple of the body has died and been laid to rest in safety. Returning to earth, the source. Are you visiting the tomb? Excavating something from the dead past? Have you finally laid something to rest? Buried it? *See* Bones; Buried; Dark; Death; Earth; Under.

TONGUE

Your ability to speak words, use language, your mother tongue. Also, to taste, to savor. *See* Eating; Food; Mute.

TOUCH

One of the five senses, touch is our sense of the physical world, our sensation, our tactile knowledge of our environment, our body. Touch has the power to heal, to soothe, to communicate, to express, to hold. It is a way to gather information.

TOWER

The Tower is aspiration and heights, the power to become visible to the world, to be seen. Is this about your hopes and plans? The construction of your ambition? From the height of the Tower we can see great distances, grasp the bigger picture. Is the Tower your ego? Your achievements? Or is your spiritual ivory tower where you hide from life in your superior isolated position? Find the Tower card in tarot and gaze at it. Don't be afraid. In tarot, lightning strikes the Tower, but I have never felt negative about this image. For me the Tower is about change. Sudden, perhaps, as is the startling swift bolt of lightning, but I have always believed in embracing change. There are many aspects to the Tower image, so take your time in pondering the meaning of this rich symbol. *See* Building; Climbing; Height; Up.

TRAIN

Riding on a train is dreaming about getting to your destination. Are you prepared, packed, ready to go? Are you on schedule? Are you running late? Your fate is predictable. The track is laid before you. Are you facing the inevitable? *See* Landscape; Weather.

TRAPPED

Are you feeling trapped, unable to break free from a habit, addiction, choice, circumstance, or relationship? Were you in the trap, or an animal? If so, look up the meaning of the animal, and think about your response to the particular animal, as it represents an aspect of your nature. *See* Bonds; Cage.

TRIANGLE

A foundation, secure and stable. The triple aspect, either body, mind, spirit; or the three faces of the Goddess, maiden, mother, or crone; the triangle is about threes, the balance of that number.

TRICKSTER

The archetypal Trickster turns up in many myths and stories. Sent to keep us humble, to tweak our ego, the Trickster will show up in unexpected impulsive behavior, or a silly mistake that embarrasses us. In dreams he reminds us not to get too full of ourselves. The power that we may wield comes *through* us, not *from* us. *See* Coyote; Flute; Fool; Magician.

TRIP

A journey; dreaming of your destination, your goal, your progress; moving to a new awareness, new ground, exploring a new world. *See* Airport; Boat; Bridge; Car; Driving; Road; Train.

TREASURE

If the treasure was hidden in your dream, and you discovered it, you are finding hidden aspects of yourself that are valuable, full of riches. A treasure symbolizes that which we prize most, our values, our inner resources, and our strengths. *See* Buried; Closet; Earth; Home/House; Key; Ocean; Under; Yard.

TREE

Associated with life and growth, roots and heritage, a tree is a living, growing, breathing entity. A beautiful image. Are you tapping into your own roots, your own heritage? Are you growing and branching out? What kind of tree was in your dream? A giving, flexible willow, or a sturdy, fatherly oak? The attributes of the tree will give you clues to its meaning for you. *See* Climbing; Earth; Evergreen; Green; Landscape; Up; Weather.

TRUCK

If you are driving the truck, you have a lot of power to get where you are going. You are taking up space, hauling forward. If the truck is behind you on the road, bearing down on you, it represents a threat, something big about to overtake you, run you down, or even off the road, off of your path. What is this threat? What kind of a truck is it? This may clue you in.

TUNNEL

Entering into the darkness of a tunnel is a classic shamanic experience, symbolizing the entry into a separate world, another reality. You may be experiencing a sort of rebirth in your spirit, a new beginning in your life, a new passage into deeper awareness. *See* Dark; Light; Road.

TURQUOISE

The aesthetic blue/green stone of the southwest that indigenous people revered for its incredible beauty, turquoise is associated with the throat chakra and enhances one's ability to use creativity expressively, to voice one's truth and spirit. Turquoise is connected to spirit and spiritual strength. *See* Crystals.

TURKEY

According to Native American symbology, a turkey symbolizes giving, the giveaway, the deep belief in giving to others, sacrificing for the good of all.

TURTLE

The turtle is an ancient symbol, sacred, associated with the land, the earth, the North American continent. It may symbolize fertility, long life, and gradual advance. Your progress may be slow, but steady.

TWINS

Representing duality, the pairing of twins may symbolize your awareness of opposites, of two sides to every aspect, dark and light, inner and outer, and so forth.

TYING

You may be tying up loose ends, finishing up, or perhaps gathering up emotions or information, pulling together the threads of facts. Tying knots can mean setting intentions, or binding.

UNDER

Going beneath the surface, getting under the apparent façade, the ego, to investigate the deeper, subconscious (under) meaning. Something hidden, unseen, not readily obvious. *See* Buried; Closet; Down; Stairs.

UP

Moving upward in a dream is revealing your progress toward your goals, toward consciousness, toward knowledge. *See* Airplane; Balcony; Climbing; Flying; Ladder; Mountain; Stairs; Wall.

URN

See Vase; Goddess.

VAGINA/VULVA

The ultimate feminine symbol, the gateway of life, the mouth of the Goddess, the Delta, the Source. The Divine Feminine. This may be a dream of worship, or integration of the Goddess into your sense of self. *See* Anima; Goddess; Lover.

VAMPIRE

The old classic vampire image instills fear, associated with the loss of blood, the draining of our vital life force. Is there something in your life that is draining your energy, your life blood? An addiction, a secret, a destructive relationship? The vampire is also seen as the Demon Lover, the ghostly addict coming to his beloved in the night to take his fill. The author Ann Rice has struck gold writing about this powerful archetype, charged with eroticism. This erotic fascination with the deadly vampire is the negative side to the attraction of the Daimon Lover. If a woman nurtures a healthy creative relationship to her inspiring inner masculine spirit, her Daimon, he fills her with the passion to create. If denied, feared, and ignored, the Daimon becomes forbidden, dark, and destructive, the archetype of the Vampire. *See* Archetypes; Anima; Animus; Blood; Daimon; Lover.

VASE

Considered a feminine symbol by virtue of being a container (often in womanly shapes), a vase can reflect your idea about your femininity, your concept of what it means to be female. An ancient urn or vase is a symbol of ancient Goddess wisdom, the container of feminine knowledge, intuition. *See* Goddess.

VEIL

A means to hide, a curtain. The veil may symbolize separation, as the veil between two worlds. *See* Curtain.

VICTIM

An aspect of yourself that identifies with playing the role of victim. In the process of growth and maturity, a Witch soon realizes that to identify with being a victim is only a half-truth. When one realizes the *power* in accepting and taking responsibility for one's own body, one's own life, one's own choices, there is a tremendous release of energy. Energy that once got lost down the hole of victimhood or martyrdom now can be rechanneled and used to invigorate other more positive experiences of life, fueling creativity, sexuality, and self-esteem. *See* Accident; Wound.

VIOLENCE

Experiencing violence in a dream should be regarded as psychic violence, symbolizing the depth of emotions fueling the dreamer's response to a person or situation. Violence can indicate rage, hurt, anger, or an aspect of yourself that has been violated, abused, trespassed. Seeing mass violence in a public arena is suggestive of the collective exposure to violence that is perpetuated and fed by the media, and your sensitivity to it. Experiencing violence in nightmares is a graphic wake-up call from the subconscious to be aware of some deep emotional issues.

VOLCANO

Dreaming of a volcano may be symbolic of a simmering emotion that you are suppressing, holding back. All that fire, all that power lies just beneath the surface of the earth, waiting to erupt at any moment. Is it anger, rage, or passion and creativity? Is it threatening, or exciting? *See* Explosion; Fire; Landscape; Mountain.

VOMITING

Purging your feelings and poisonous negative emotions such as anger, rage, or hurt can be a liberating experience, and our subconscious allows us to do it in dreams symbolically by vomiting it all out in a dream state; we can purify ourselves without actually harming the object of our anger and rage. *See* Bathroom; Food.

WALL

A wall is built in defense or for protection and symbolizes the inner walls we build to protect our ego, our insecurity, our sense of safety. Were you building a wall in your dream, or tearing one down? Climbing over a wall can indicate that you are willing to scale an obstacle standing in your way toward consciousness. *See* Building; Climbing; Landscape; Renovate; Window.

WALLET

A wallet contains proof of our identity, our self-worth: driver's license, credit cards, identification, as well as what we value (money). Have you lost your wallet in the dream? Are you losing your sense of self-worth, your identity? Are you searching for it? Do you feel lost without your wallet, your proof of who you are in the world? Are you authentic? Do you feel as if you *are* who you say you are? *See* Coins; Purse.

WAND

An extension of the Witch's power, a wand extends the arm and hand from which the Witch projects energy, focus, and intent. If you dream of using your wand to affect change, you are tapping into your power, realizing your ability. Wands are also associated with the element of fire. Look up the suit of Wands in tarot, and meditate on further meaning. *See* Lightning; Magician; Witch; Wizard.

WATCH

Looking at a watch may symbolize your awareness of (calendar) time or the pressure of a schedule. Do you feel as if you are running late, losing time, or don't have *enough* time? Is it a simple play on words? To "watch out"?

WAR

Dreaming of war is dreaming of conflict, the scale of which is reflected in the dream: from a battle to full-blown war. Are you feeling conflicted somewhere in your life? Are you doing battle with yourself? Or do you feel at *war* with the collective, or your family? The bloodier the images, the more damage is being sustained by you in this conflict. The more blood lost, the more life energy is being wasted in this battle. The price is high. *See* Blood; Collective; Soldier; Violence.

WASHING

Cleansing and purifying are aspects of washing. Are you in a process of growth that is prompting you to wash away your mistakes, your past, old negativity, unwanted parts of your life, yourself? Do you wish you could begin anew, fresh, cleansed? Try an actual purification bath with sea salts and appropriate essential oils to ritualize your dream image. *See* Water.

WATER

One of the four elements, water represents the realm of emotions. The depths of our subconscious mind. Water is our origins and our sustenance. Without water, we perish. Likewise, emotions are life-sustaining, cleansing, and healing. Emotions take physical form in the emergence of tears. We cry in grief and in joy, both are spontaneous fluid expressions of our inner emotions. We give birth with a gush of water, again a reminder of our aquatic roots. Water is life, sacred and healing. *See* Lake; Ocean; River; Washing; Waves.

WAVES

Rising waves are evidence of swelling emotions. If the waves are turbulent, rocking, the emotions are strong and possibly threatening; if the waves are gentle, these are emotions we can easily handle. Are you able to ride the waves in your dream? *Being* the wave is symbolic of understanding that "all is connected," that each of us is a wave, a part of the whole ocean of life. *See* Anchor; Boat; Lake; Ocean; Water.

WEATHER

The weather in your dream will give you a clue as to the state of your emotional environment. If it is clear and sunny, you are in expansive, conscious territory. If the weather is stormy, you are unsettled and experiencing turbulence. Snow and ice are indicative of the lack of emotions; frozen water is frozen response, static and glacial, cut off from the depths of water running freely. Dry desert can indicate an arid lack of life energy; you are parched, thirsty for life-quenching experience, perhaps cut off from your juicier sensuality or feeling deserted. *See* Landscape.

WEASEL

Not commonly revered, the weasel is usually associated with slick slippery ethics and a lack of responsibility. He is also the messenger of information; being the stealthy character that he is, he often gets the scoop on what's really going on by hanging out on the fringes and listening with keen observation. (Are you in need of this trait?) Or is this warning that someone in your life is about to betray your trust by divulging information about you? We've all known a few weasels in our time. *See* Archetype.

WEDDING

Preparing for a wedding is the classic dream of preparing for our inner union, our integration: embracing our opposite, the Anima or Animus, uniting with our shadow, accepting ourselves as whole. As the path to becoming an authentic individual progresses, we will have more frequent dreams of marrying, choosing our wedding dress and attire, traveling toward the ceremony. "On the way to the wedding" dreams exemplify Jung's concept of health = wholeness. The union of all of our aspects, the acceptance of all of our various selves, light and dark. The path to maturity is the path toward integration, toward balance, toward oneness. *See* Anima; Animus; Archetype; Clothing; Lover; Marriage.

WELL

An ancient symbol of the Goddess, the feminine divine, the well represents access to deep waters, to the dark mysteries of the earth, to a life-giving underground reservoir. The sacred well is the life-sustaining way of the Goddess. *See* Chalice; Cup; Earth; Goddess; Water.

WHALE

Being warm-blooded mammals, whales are ancient creatures of the living sea—enormous, maternal, warm. They represent the ancient feminine, the Goddess in her primal energy, surviving in the dark depths of the collective unconscious. A whale dream is a gift from the feminine divine. *See* Goddess; Ocean; Water.

WHEEL

For pagans, the wheel symbolizes the turning seasons, based on eight points of the year. Celebrating the earth's relationship to the sun are the solar festivals: the Spring Equinox and Autumn Equinox, when the daylight and darkness is in equal balance; the Summer Solstice, the year's longest day; and Winter Solstice, the year's longest night. The moon is celebrated at the four lunar festivals: Imbolc, in early February, the crescent waxing moon; Beltane on May 1, the full moon; Lughnasadh on August 1, the waning moon; and Samhain (Hallow's Eve) on October 31, the dark moon. Reflecting the sacredness of the cycle or circle, wheels and circles are expressions of the divine order in nature and our active participation in her spiral way. *See* Archetype; Circle; Earth; God; Goddess; Seasons.

WIFE

If you are dreaming of your actual wife, you may be dreaming of your projected feminine self, the inner woman, your Anima. Men often project their own inner feminine onto their wife and expect her to carry it for them, to express their female side for them. If you have a more integrated balanced self and have worked on incorporating your own feminine aspects, you may be dreaming of the real marriage, your relationship. You must decide if the dream is about you, your inner workings, or the marriage, how you relate within the partnership. *See* Archetype; Anima; Husband; Lover; Marriage; Muse.

WIND

Associated with air and spirit, wind is the air element, the breath of the Goddess. She is movement and change. *See* Air; Feather; Wings.

WINDOW

A glimpse to the outside, a view toward consciousness, light. A window may also be a *window of opportunity.* A time frame, an opening to another awareness. *See* Curtains; Daylight; House; Light; Renovate; Room.

WINE

Sacred to the God and Goddess, wine is the fruit of the vine, the *spirit,* the blood, the holy. A gift from the Gods, wine is healing, curative, and celebrational. *See* Alcohol; Cup; Chalice; Drink.

WINGS

Containing the ability to fly, to soar above, to reach heights, the realm of the sky, spirit, spiritual aspirations. Perhaps you have angelic associations. *See* Air; Birds; Eagles; Feather; Flying; Sky.

WITCH

Once revered as Wise Woman and Healer, Medicine Woman, and the One Who Knows, the Woman Who Lives in the Woods has always been a part of our collective myth. In the past several centuries, with the domination of the patriarchal Christian church, the archetypal Witch has been denigrated, feared, and persecuted. During the Middle Ages she became a scapegoat for the collective fears of men in power (especially those in medicine and religion) who perhaps envied and condemned her knowledge of herbs, healing, and midwifery. But any woman of independence and self-taught knowledge was suspect. The poorer country folks' adherence to the Old Folk Ways was viewed as a threat to the segregated male power of the church, in bed with corrupt politicians. Those who loved the Goddess quietly challenged the church's doctrine of a masculine image of the Godhead. Many innocents and simple people were persecuted as Witches and forced to confess to practices that were nothing more than prurient fantasies of unbalanced men in power. Yet the Witch has survived. She has persevered in spite of the church's Inquisition and negative propaganda, in spite of vicious local Witch hunts, even in America, a mere two hundred years ago. She has survived. Yes, her archetype of the once respected Wise Woman has been altered, disparaged by the fear-filled projections of the Christian church's destructive teachings. Ironically, as literacy expanded to the common people, it got worse. The written word began to replace ancient folk knowledge and reliance on intuition, and the prevailing collective exiled the Witch in the name of science and reason. Later she emerged in fairy tales to embody moralistic illustrations of evil, complete with warty nose and a black pointy hat (actually thought to be early Christian garb), flying on her broomstick and cooking up lost children for supper. Yet, still, our beloved Witch survives.

She is now quietly living in every community, working with herbs and the phases of the moon, revering the earth and following the Old Ways of the Goddess. If the Witch has appeared in your dreams, she may be reflecting to you her surviving truth, her phoenixlike Wise Woman archetype, perhaps to become your personal inner guide. If she appears ugly and frightening, she is reflecting your fear, especially if you view her as the collective's embodiment of evil. She is then merely your own fear taking form, your shadow trying to get your attention. (If you are a man dreaming of the negative evil Witch, you are being confronted with your dark feminine side, your shadowy Anima.) How you dream the Witch is a reflection on your own spirit. She is holding up a mirror to you. *See* Anima; Archetype.

WIZARD

The archetype of the Wise Old Man, the Druid, Merlin, the Magician, Medicine Man. Interestingly, the male counterpart to the Witch archetype has not suffered nearly the indignity of the Witch. We still collectively view him with respect and a bit of awe. (Certainly there were men who were persecuted for witchcraft as well during the middle ages, but not nearly to the extent that women and children were targeted and murdered.) His appearance in your dream may indicate an emergence of such old wisdom within yourself. He may be a guide to your true path. *See* Archetype; Magician; Witch.

WOLF

A powerful and popular animal totem, the wolf symbolizes keen awareness; his ally is the light of the moon. The wolf is a pathfinder and a teacher. If a wolf has come to you in your dreams, you may indeed have wolf medicine. Read up on the wolf and his nature, and invite him to be your animal ally.

WOMAN

See Anima; Muse; Lover; Shadow.

WOODS

See Forest.

WOUND

A physical wounding in a dream is evidence of an emotional wound or psychic injury. How did you receive this wound? And where were you hurt, what part of the body? This will give you a clue as to what function was wounded in you; for example: hand—the ability to grasp, to make; heart—the ability to feel, to love; throat—the ability to speak your own truth, express who you are. Does your wound define who you are? Do you overly identify with your wound? *See* Bandage; Battle; Blood.

WRITE

To write in a dream is to formulate words to express yourself. Usually, upon waking, the dreamer will not be able to remember what was written or read. The half of the brain that uses language and letters, writing and math, is the left half of the brain; the logical, more linear half. The opposite side of the brain, the right, is the half where images and symbols, intuition and feelings dominate. Our dreaming takes place in a state most conducive to this right brain, communicating to us directly in symbolic language. That is why it is so often helpful to write your dreams down with your nondominant hand, utilizing the opposite side of the brain to connect more directly with your dream images. *See* Books; Library.

X-RAY

Having an x-ray is a way to examine within, to see beyond the outer surface. If you are looking at an x-ray in your dream, you are holding up an aspect of your inner self to examine it, bring it to light, see beneath the exterior. *See* Bones; Hospital; Medicine.

YARD

A share of your house environment, the yard can be seen as an extension of your sense of self. It is a clue to your emotional environment, your psychic space, your family influences, your childhood arena (if it is the family yard of your childhood). What are you doing in your yard? How do feel there? *See* Home/House; Landscape.

YELLOW

The color of the sun, bright, cheerful. Yellow is associated with creativity, happiness, and healing energy.

YOUTH

A youth may symbolize the immature aspect of yourself or, if the youth is the opposite sex, the immature Anima or Animus. If the dream is accompanied by longing or searching, you may be trying to recover a lost part of your youth, your younger self, something that you have discarded along the road to adulthood, a childhood dream, perhaps? *See* Anima; Animus; Archetype; Child.

ZOMBIE

The walking dead, a zombie may indicate that you feel as if you are sleepwalking through your existence, without vital life energy, deadened. This is a frightening dream image. Are you in need of some life-giving nurturing experience? Have you been taking care of your body and your spirit? Take the time to make some positive changes that will fill you and sustain you. *See* Buried; Death; Grave.

ZOO

How do you feel about zoos? Some dreamers may feel strongly negative about them, sensitive to the entrapment of the once-wild animals who have just as much of a right to exist freely on this planet as we humans do. Other dreamers may only have a pleasant childhood memory of a day at the zoo, with balloons and cotton candy. Examine your own personal associations to this image. *See* Animals.

APPENDIX A

CORRESPONDENCES

In working with dreams and magick, a Witch needs to familiarize herself with the meanings of the four elements and their magickal correspondences. For instance, recognizing a season, a tarot symbol, or a color within your dreamscape may reveal a thread of clues. Once you determine the association of a dream symbol, find the correspondences and work intuitively with their meanings.

If you find that you are dreaming about winter, for example, you may be dealing with a question regarding the earth element. The correspondences show us that winter is feminine energy, a time for grounding, not growth. Are you tending to such needs in your life? Work with the herbal and color correspondences in a ritual bath or meditation. Make a body lotion scented with the grounding oils of patchouli, pine, and orange. Study the suit of Pentacles in tarot, and use your intuition to respond to the individual cards. Do you need to learn patience? Are you craving more stability? Your intuition will guide you to the answers as you work with these correspondences on a regular basis.

On the following page is a chart showing the associations linked to the four elements, their direction, season, and attributes. I have also included their associations for magickal intentions, suits in tarot, colors, and herbal energy equivalents, for Craft work.

	Earth	Air	Fire	Water
Direction	North	East	South	West
Season	Winter	Spring	Summer	Autumn
Attributes	Feminine	Masculine	Masculine	Feminine
	Passive/Static	Active	Active	Passive/Fluid
	Matter/Body	Mental	Physical	Emotional/Psychic
Magickal	Grounding	Communication	Cleansing	Death
	Wisdom	Protection	Transformation	Rebirth
	Patience	Education	Creative Impulse	Psychic/Intuition
	Stability	Intention	Protection	Divination
Tarot	Pentacles	Swords	Wands	Cups
Colors	White/Green	Yellow	Red	Black/Blue
Herbs/Oils	Pine	Rosemary	Cinnamon	Lavender
	Patchouli	Lavender	Ginger	Jasmine
	Cedar	Sage	Basil	Cypress Bark
	Juniper	Mugwort	Garlic	Moss
	Oak	Spearmint	Thyme	Vanilla
	Orange Peel	Wormwood	Peppermint	Honeysuckle

Correspondences

APPENDIX B

CHAKRAS

The seven chakra centers in the body, also known as energy gateways, correspond to seven spiritual-soul lessons. Energy may become blocked when corresponding issues are ignored or violated, and physical symptoms may develop within that body area. Dreams may warn of blockages in the chakras with imagery that ties in to the specific area of the body. For instance, one may dream of a gash to the throat, indicating an issue about speaking one's truth, finding one's own voice.

One dreamer I knew dreamt of black boxes stuck in his abdomen. He had been wounded by an abusive childhood; his experience of family origins being untrustworthy, even harmful, had blocked his lower chakras, and his energy was stuck there, stagnant, confining him to a constant state of depression.

Meditate to encourage your own chakra healing, visualizing the appropriate color for each energy center.

Sit quietly and breathe deeply. Close your eyes. Begin with the first chakra, the root chakra, seeing the deep red and orange colors glow at the base of your spine, and slowly move up through the body, visualizing each chakra bathed in the corresponding healing color. Remember to *breathe!*

Appendix B

ROOT CHAKRA

The first chakra. At the low, deep base of the spine, the first chakra represents your link to the physical world, your origins, your tribal connections. The participation in the collective. Group mind. *Color: Red/Deep Orange*.

LOWER ABDOMEN CHAKRA

The second chakra. Your seat of emotions, sexuality, and creativity. "Gut feelings." The center of your internal fire. *Color: Orange*.

SOLAR PLEXUS CHAKRA

The third chakra. This is the location of personality, the center where feeling and being are integrated. The diaphragm, seat of breath, life, and the awareness I am and I desire. *Color: Yellow*.

HEART CHAKRA

The fourth chakra. Your heart (chest area and back/shoulder blades) is the seat of transformation, where the creative impulse becomes emotion. Feelings become compassion. The gateway of empathy. *Color: Green*.

THROAT CHAKRA

The fifth chakra. The throat is the gateway for self-expression. Speaking one's truth. Communication. *Color: Blue*.

THIRD EYE CHAKRA

The sixth chakra. The eye of "knowing." Your awareness of the psychic realm; recognition of other realities. *Color: Indigo*.

CROWN CHAKRA

The seventh chakra. Aptly named, the crown chakra, the top of the head, connects the individual to the truths of the universe. Keeping the flow of energy free allows the divine life force to enter and inspire with universal truth. *Color: Purple*.

BIBLIOGRAPHY

Bolen, Jean Shinoda. *Goddesses in Everywoman: A New Psychology of Women.* San Francisco, Calif.: Harper & Row, Publishers, 1984.

———. *Gods in Everyman: A New Psychology of Men's Lives and Loves.* San Francisco, Calif.: Harper & Row, Publishers, 1989.

Black Elk, Wallace. *Black Elk: The Sacred Ways of a Lakota.* New York: HarperCollins Publishers, 1990.

Bly, Robert. *A Little Book on the Human Shadow.* New York: Harper & Row Publishers, Inc., 1988.

Bradley, Marion Zimmer. *The Mists of Avalon.* New York: Ballantine Books, 1982.

Campbell, Joseph, with Bill Moyers. *The Power of Myth.* New York: Doubleday, 1988.

———. *Transformations of Myth Through Time.* New York: Harper & Row Publishers, Inc., 1990.

Claremont de Castillejo, Irene. *Knowing Woman: A Feminine Psychology.* New York: Harper & Row Publishers, Inc., 1973.

Donner, Florinda. *Being-In-Dreaming: An Initiation Into the Sorcerers' World.* New York: HarperCollins Publishers, 1991.

Farrar, Janet and Stewart. *The Witches' Goddess.* Blaine, Wash.: Phoenix Publishing Inc., 1987.

Fontana, David. *The Secret Language of Symbols.* San Francisco, Calif.: Chronicle Books, 1993.

Franklin, Anna. *The Sacred Circle Tarot: A Celtic Pagan Journey.* St. Paul, Minn.: Llewellyn Publications, 1998.

Galenorn, Yasmine. *Tarot Journeys.* St. Paul, Minn.: Llewellyn Publications, 1999.

George, Demetra. *Mysteries of the Dark Moon: The Healing Power of the Dark Goddess.* San Francisco, Calif.: HarperSanFrancisco, 1992.

Green, Marion. *A Witch Alone: Thirteen Moons to Master Natural Magic*. London: Thorsons, An Imprint of HarperCollins Publishers, 1991.

Hopman, Ellen Evert. *A Druid's Herbal for the Sacred Earth Year*. Rochester, Vt.: Destiny Books, a division of Inner Traditions, 1995.

Johnson, Robert A. *He: Understanding Masculine Psychology*. New York: Harper & Row Publishers, Inc., 1974.

———. *Inner Work: Using Dreams and Active Imagination for Personal Growth*. New York: HarperCollins Publishers, 1986.

———. *Owning Your Own Shadow: Understanding The Dark Side of the Psyche*. New York: HarperCollins, 1991.

———. *She: Understanding Feminine Psychology*. New York: Harper & Row Publishers, Inc., 1976.

Jung, C. G. *Dreams*. Princeton, N.J.: Princeton University Press, 1974.

———. *Memories, Dreams, Reflections*. New York: Random House, 1965.

———. *Man and his Symbols*. New York: Doubleday, 1964.

Kennealy, Patricia. *Strange Days: My Life with and without Jim Morrison*. New York: Penguin Group, Penguin Books, 1993.

Leonard, Linda Schierse. *On The Way To The Wedding*. Boston, Mass.: Shambhala, 1986.

———. *The Wounded Woman: Healing The Father-Daughter Relationship*. Boston, Mass.: Shambhala, 1982.

Manzarek, Ray. *Light My Fire: My Life with the Doors*. New York: Berkley Boulevard Books, Berkley Publishing Group, 1999.

Mascetti, Manuela Dunn. *The Song of Eve: An Illustrated Journey Into the Myths, Symbols, and Rituals of the Goddess*. New York: Simon & Schuster, Inc., 1990.

Matthews, Caitlin. *The Search of Woman's Passionate Soul: Revealing the Daimon Lover Within*. Rockport, Mass.: Element Books, Inc., 1997.

Mindell, Arnold. *Dreambody: The Body's Role in Revealing the Self*. Portland, Oreg.: Lao Tse Press, 1998.

Moore, Robert, and Douglas Gillette. *King Warrior Magician Lover: Rediscovering the Archetypes of the Mature Masculine*. New York: HarperCollins, 1990.

Moura, Ann (Aoumiel). *Green Witchcraft: Folk Magic, Fairy Lore & Herb Craft*. St. Paul, Minn.: Llewellyn Publications, 1996.

———. *Green Witchcraft II: Balancing Light & Shadow*. St. Paul, Minn.: Llewellyn Publications, 1999.

Murdock, Maureen. *The Heroine's Journey: Woman's Quest for Wholeness*. Boston, Mass.: Shambhala, 1990.

Myss, Caroline. *Anatomy of the Spirit; The Seven Stages of Power and Healing*. New York: Harmony Books, 1996.

Neihardt, John G. *Black Elk Speaks: Being the Life Story of a Holy Man of the Oglala Sioux*. Lincoln, Nebr.: University of Nebraska Press, 1961.

Bibliography

Nichols, Sallie. *Jung and Tarot: An Archetypal Journey*. York Beach, Maine: Samuel Weiser, 1980.

Paglia, Camille. *Vamps and Tramps: New Essays*. New York: Vintage Books, Random House, 1994.

Perera, Sylvia Brinton. *Descent to the Goddess: A Way of Initiation for Women*. Toronto, Canada: Inner City Books, 1981.

Stein, Diane. *All Women Are Healers*. Freedom, Calif.: The Crossing Press, 1990.

Vogler, Christopher. *The Writer's Journey: Mythic Structure for Writers*. Studio City, Calif.: Michael Wiese Productions, 1998.

von Franz, Marie-Louise. *On Dreams & Death*. Boston, Mass.: Shambhala Publications, Inc., 1986.

Voytilla, Stuart. *Myth and the Movies: Discovering the Mythic Structure of 50 Unforgettable Films*. Studio City, Calif.: Michael Wiese Productions, 1999.

Walker, Barbara G. *The Woman's Dictionary of Symbols and Sacred Objects*. New York: HarperCollins Publishers, 1988.

Weinstein, Marion. *Positive Magic: Occult Self Help*. New York: Earth Magic Productions, Inc., 1978.

Woodman, Marion. *Conscious Femininity: Interviews with Marion Woodman*. Toronto: Inner City Books, 1993.

Woodman, Marion. *Dancing in the Flames: The Dark Goddess in the Transformation of Consciousness*. Boston, Mass.: Shambhala, 1996.

Woodman, Marion, with Kate Danson, Mary Hamilton, Rita Greer Allen. *Leaving My Father's House: A Journey to Conscious Femininity*. Boston, Mass.: Shambhala, 1992.

Worth, Valerie. *Crone's Book of Charms and Spells*. St. Paul, Minn.: Llewellyn Publications, 1999.

Zweig, Connie, and Jeremiah Abrams. *Meeting the Shadow: The Hidden Power of the Dark Side of Human Nature*. New York: Jeremy P. Tarcher/Putnam, Penguin Putman, Inc., 1991.

INDEX

Index

blood, 3, 31, 39, 45, 47, 51, 67, 70, 110, 114, 128, 169, 191, 202, 204–205, 208, 210

body, 1, 49, 52, 73, 75, 78–79, 91, 105, 121, 125, 130, 133, 143, 148, 151, 153, 156, 158, 160, 171–172, 175, 182, 186, 197–199, 202, 210, 212

bodywork, 20, 28

Bono, 29–30

Braveheart, 6–7, 15

bride, 16, 32, 36–37

Bull Durham, 12, 15

Burton, Tim, 13

celebrity, 21, 108

Celtic, 4, 32, 42, 91, 114, 121, 126–127, 134, 158, 171

chakra, 47, 115, 121, 145–148, 160, 169, 173, 179, 197, 200

Channing, Stockard, 13

characters, 3, 13, 15, 17, 21, 39

child, 3, 17–20, 23, 29, 38–39, 59, 90–91, 109, 117, 122, 129, 143, 155, 169, 174, 212

childhood, 3, 5, 17–20, 22, 35, 45–46, 52, 55, 86, 96, 140–141, 155, 166, 193, 211–212

Christian, 43, 61, 108, 127, 150–151, 179, 192, 208–209

Christian church, 43, 61, 208–209

Christian devil, 151

Cinderella, 13

climbing, 6, 52, 70, 78, 110, 123, 144, 148–149, 158, 167, 175, 198–199, 201, 203–204

Clooney, George, 12

Close, Glenn, 38

clothing, 20, 119, 123, 184, 206

clown, 3–4, 108, 124

coins, 97, 119, 124, 130, 132, 144, 165, 176, 178, 180, 204

collective, 1–2, 6, 10–15, 20, 25, 33–35, 37–38, 43–45, 47, 52, 57–59, 61, 63–64, 66–67, 70–75, 78–79, 81–82, 87, 89–90, 96, 99, 103, 107–109, 113, 122, 124–125, 135–136, 140–141, 143–146, 151, 154–155, 162, 164–165, 171, 177, 181, 185, 187, 193, 203–205, 207–209

Collective Unconscious, 2, 14–15, 108, 171, 207

colors, 21, 79, 125, 185

comfort zone, 49

comics, 9, 108

conflict, 70, 73, 108, 111–112, 124, 137, 157, 204

conform, 15, 20, 59, 96, 124–125, 155, 193

consciousness, 5–6, 19, 32, 34, 37, 60, 62, 64, 69, 95, 110, 128–129, 134, 150, 158, 160, 162, 168, 176–177, 194, 196, 201, 204, 208

control, 22–26, 34, 39, 47, 120, 131, 135, 140, 151, 165, 169, 179

corporation, 37

correspondences, 77, 80, 121, 127

creativity, 11, 19, 27–28, 30–32, 37, 51–52, 58, 63–64, 73, 83, 106, 128, 148, 168, 173, 200, 203, 211

creature, 53, 63, 129, 172

Cups, Suit of, 12–13

Cusack, John, 12

Daimon Lover, 11, 28, 30, 32, 57, 75, 93, 106–107, 128, 152, 156, 161–162, 176, 188, 202

dark, 3, 8, 12, 14, 26–28, 30–31, 38, 48, 56–58, 60–68, 70, 73–75, 107, 110–111, 114, 118, 120–121, 124, 129, 131, 140, 146, 149, 151, 154, 156, 162, 166, 168, 170, 172, 174, 178, 182, 188, 197, 200–202, 206–207, 209

Index

Index

Index

Index

Index

Index